Published in 2003 by I.B.Tauris & Co Ltd
6 Salem Road, London W2 4BU
175 Fifth Avenue, New York NY 10010
www.ibtauris.com

In the United States and Canada distributed by Palgrave Macmillan,
a division of St. Martin's Press
175 Fifth Avenue, New York NY 10010

ISBN 1 86064 897 5

A full CIP record for this book is available from the British Library
A full CIP record for this book is available from the Library of Congress

Typeset in Minion by Dexter Haven Associates, London
Printed and bound in Great Britain by MPG Books, Bodmin

CONTENTS

Illustrations. iv

Preface. v

PART I: THE CIVIL WAR

  1 The Romance Begins 3

  2 The Germans and Ludwig Blenker 15

  3 The 8th New York Volunteers. 22

  4 The 68th New York Volunteers. 34

  5 Brigadier General Felix Prince Salm 59

PART II: MEXICO

  6 Maximilian, Emperor of Mexico 69

  7 Querétaro 80

  8 Agnes Goes on the Offensive 93

  9 The Prisoners 100

  10 Felix Rescued 118

PART III: GERMANY

  11 Settling In 129

  12 Back in Service 139

  13 The Franco–Prussian War. 150

Epilogue – The Later Years. 175

Notes on the Text 190

Bibliography 193

Index. 197

ILLUSTRATIONS

1 Agnes Leclerq Joy was a vivacious 20-year-old who in 1861 was already making her mark on Washington society (Collection of the Atlanta History Center).

2 Prince Felix zu Salm-Salm came to America to seek his military fortune (Studio of Matthew Brady, Collection of the New York Historical Society).

3 Felix became Colonel of the 8th New York Volunteers following energetic lobbying by his bride Agnes. He fought bravely in the Civil War (Collection of the New York Historical Society).

4 Agnes deployed her prodigious energy towards medical relief work in the Civil War (Collection of the Atlanta History Center).

5 The *Atlanta Journal*, very much a Southern newspaper, had an indulgent view of the Salms, not least because while Felix was military governor of the city he and Agnes had a benevolent view of the defeated South.

6 Emperor Maximilian of Mexico was able to count heavily on the loyalty of Felix, though the attempts of Agnes to save him from execution did not succeed (Culver Pictures Inc.).

7 Schloss Anholt, family seat of the Salms in Prussia, was a forbidding place for the exuberant Agnes (author's photograph).

8 King Wilhelm I of Prussia (later Emperor of Germany) grew fond of Agnes (Culver Pictures Inc.).

9 Queen (later Empress) Augusta was a generous friend to Agnes, the German Princess from America (Culver Pictures Inc.).

10 Agnes, portrayed here by Franz Winterhalter, attempted to remain socially active following the death of Felix (Foto Marburg).

PREFACE

While re-reading Sybille Bedford's *A Visit to Don Otavio*, a memoir of her time in Mexico in the 1950s, I came across a reference to the heroic efforts of the American-born Princess Agnes Salm to save Emperor Maximilian of Mexico from execution in 1867. Her book *Ten Years of My Life* was cited in the bibliography, and I headed off to the New York Public Library to see if I could find it. I did, along with Prince Felix's own story of his experiences in Mexico. Reading them, I knew I had found the makings of what my grandmother used to call a rattling good yarn.

Agnes Joy, born in a small town on the Vermont–Quebec border, was an extraordinary woman. She was beautiful, vivacious, absolutely fearless and more than a little courageous. When she set her mind on something, nothing could stand in her way. She never wasted time with underlings, but went straight to the top: senators, governors, cabinet ministers and presidents all succumbed in their turn to her charms and persuasions. She scandalised many but captivated many more, and those she captivated were more important than those she scandalised.

Her fortunes were at a low ebb in the summer of 1861 when she met Prince Felix zu Salm-Salm, a Prussian officer in Union service at the outbreak of the American Civil War. He himself had left Germany pursued by debts run up by high living. They were soon wed, and she made his cause hers. She schemed and connived to secure him the command of first one New York volunteer regiment and then another, and before she was finished in 1865 Felix was a brigadier-general and in command of the Atlanta Military District, an impressive feat for the wife of a young Prussian officer. She accompanied him in his Civil War career, and pitched in to army life with gusto.

The Civil War over, Felix turned to Mexico to fight for the beleaguered Emperor Maximilian. He fought bravely in the siege of Querétaro, and was captured along with the emperor when the city fell to the forces of Benito Juárez. Condemned to be shot, Maximilian had few more tireless admirers than Agnes, who did more than any other human being to try to save him. Even the implacable Juárez was moved; not enough, but she had done her best. Felix, too, was condemned to die, but was eventually released.

The couple returned to Germany, to the Salm ancestral castle. The Salm connections gave Agnes ready access to the upper ranks of German society. King Wilhelm of Prussia, later German Emperor, and Queen Augusta treated her with great kindness. Tragically, just as she had settled down to the first really normal life she had known, Felix was cut down in the opening weeks of the Franco–Prussian War in 1870.

Beyond all the glamour, Agnes had a profoundly humanitarian side. The treatment of battlefield casualties was primitive in 1861, and she devoted herself to seeing that hospital care reached those who needed it most. The skills she honed in the Civil War were perfected in her field-hospital work during the Franco–Prussian War, and she was awarded the highest honour the emperor could manage for a woman who had done so much in a field traditionally dominated by men. Despite her titles and privileges, she was a woman of great compassion, and she never shied from rolling up her sleeves and getting her hands dirty when there was work to be done.

By all accounts, theirs was a happy marriage, their very different backgrounds and natures notwithstanding. Felix was the improvident younger son of an ancient German noble family who was good at one thing only – being a soldier. He was headstrong and brave, not always a good combination. Agnes was a more complicated person. She was desperate to escape the uncertainties and struggles of her early years, and saw in Felix the way to do it. Her ambitions for him, and for her, were boundless, and she used every trick in the book to get what she wanted. She rarely failed. She was undoubtedly a good bit more clever than Felix, but without him she would never have accomplished what she did. From being a mid-Western circus performer to dining at the royal courts of Europe was quite a voyage! Let us follow her.

PART I

The Civil War

1

The Romance Begins

It was a fine autumn day in Washington. Perfect for an outing to the army camps, a popular pastime since Union troops had occupied the Virginia side of the Potomac River, opposite the capital. A gaily dressed throng of ladies and gentlemen clattered by horse and carriage over the Long Bridge that ran from the foot of Maryland Avenue across the river. Among them were Agnes Leclerq Joy, her sister Delia and Delia's husband Lt Edmund Johnson, down from New York to enjoy the parades and military reviews laid on by General George B. McClellan, the new Union commander.

Following the unexpected and shocking rout of Union troops at Bull Run on 21 July 1861, the first real test of arms in the Civil War, the popular young McClellan had been summoned to take over from the unfortunate commanders who were blamed for the Union defeat. McClellan plunged swiftly into the task of organising the capital's defences, and in August formed the new Army of the Potomac. Drills and parades helped whip the recruits into shape and instil a sense of purpose and direction sadly lacking theretofore. The complacency of previous weeks was giving way to the realisation that tough days lay ahead. The McClellan reviews were immensely popular, and did much to restore Union morale. Nothing like them had been seen in anyone's lifetime, and people came from far and wide.

Abraham Lincoln had been sworn in as sixteenth president on 4 March 1861. The long-simmering dispute between the slave and free states had come to a head in December 1860 when South Carolina seceded from the Union. Most of the other Southern states followed suit in January and February 1861 to form the Confederate States of America, and on 12 April Southern guns opened fire on Federal Fort Sumter in the harbour of Charleston, South Carolina. The war had begun.

Washington was virtually surrounded by hostile territory. Virginia and Maryland had not yet seceded, but their people were strongly secessionist in sympathy. Most of the small US regular army – some 15,000 strong in 1861 – was out West fighting Indians and providing military support for America's relentless expansion toward the Pacific coast. The only serious war it had fought had been with Mexico between 1846 and 1848; that was the sole military experience for the bulk of the general officers. Besides, reliance on volunteer state militias, not a standing army, was the American tradition.

On 14 April, the President called for 75,000 volunteers to serve for three months. It was widely assumed in the North that the rebellion would soon be put down. The state governors responded with alacrity to recruit their quotas of regiments. Excitement was at fever pitch, and volunteer units soon poured into the city. Two weeks later, Lincoln called for an additional 42,000 men to serve for three years. When Virginia voted to secede on 23 May, the Federal government occupied Arlington Heights, Alexandria and a strip of land in Virginia across the Potomac. It was not until July 1862 that the President called for another 300,000 volunteers, and only in 1863 was conscription – the draft – introduced.

Lincoln grasped all too well the enormity of the task before him, but in the popular mind, and to too many in the government, it was all something of a lark. When rumours of an impending battle reached the capital that second week in July, a horde of people, including congressmen and other officials, went out to see the show. Bull Run was a scant 25 miles from downtown Washington. Many correspondents described the picnic hampers, the champagne and the general merriment. When the rout began, the civilians were caught up in the debacle and swept back into the capital bruised and dusty. A congressman from New York was captured.

The hero of Bull Run was Colonel Louis Blenker, a German-born officer whose brigade, held in reserve at the rear, had stood firm as the Union forces tumbled back into Washington. Fortunately for the Union, the Confederate forces were equally exhausted and almost as green as its own, and were thus unable to follow up their victory. In any case, Colonel Blenker's brigade was widely credited with having saved the day. Agnes was a trifle sceptical, observing that such had been the danger that the people exaggerated Blenker's contribution. Blenker himself, she wrote, 'did not overrate it, but was sensible enough to profit by this temporary tide of popular favour'.

In November, Blenker's brigade of some 12,000 men moved to Hunter's Chapel, a few miles south of the Long Bridge, toward Alexandria. His camp was famous for its glitter and hospitality, and there Agnes and the Johnsons were headed. They were received most cordially.

> We had not long been there when we heard the sentinels present arms, and the curtain at the entrance of the tent was thrown back. An officer entered, returning from an inspection of the outposts, reporting to the General, who then presented him to the ladies as the chief of his staff – Colonel Prince Salm.

Agnes was smitten at once, and so, apparently, was Colonel Salm. She wrote,

> He was of middle height, had an elegant figure, dark hair, light moustache, and a very agreeable handsome face, the kind and modest expression of which was highly prepossessing. He had very fine dark eyes, which, however, seemed not to be very good, as he had to use a glass [monocle], which he perpetually wore in his right eye, managing it with all the skill of a Prussian officer of the guard.
>
> I felt particularly attracted to the face of the Prince, and it was evident that my face had the same effect on him. He addressed me in his polite and smiling manner, but, alas, he did not speak one word of English, and as I did not understand either German or French, and only very imperfectly Spanish, of which he had some superficial knowledge, our conversation would have been very unsatisfactory without the assistance of the more universal language of the eyes, which both of us understood much better.

When she left Blenker's camp, she continued, 'I left behind an enamoured Prince, whose feelings were far from being indifferent to me. We saw each other again; the sweet malady increased, and the Prince proposed.' They were married on 30 August 1862 in a Catholic ceremony at St Patrick's Church in Washington. It was the same day that the Union suffered another major defeat at the Second Battle of Bull Run.

The day of disaster for the Union had proved a day of triumph for Agnes. Never a sentimental lightweight, the young woman from a humble background, recently arrived in New York from Havana with limited prospects at best, had transformed herself into a princess. Her description of the whirlwind romance and courtship is a trifle glib, but she obviously saw in Felix a chance to improve her rather doubtful circumstances, and she set her cap for him. Then, too, Agnes had had a rather loveless life so far, and this was her chance at last.

As for Felix, he must have seen in this lovely and beguiling girl an opportunity for happiness that he could not let slip. He too had escaped difficulties at home and was seeking his way in a land far different from what he had known. At last, he had connected. He had found someone to guide him through the shoals of life in America. He also must have set himself briskly to learning English. Agnes spoke of their lively correspondence while she was in Washington and he in the field, conducted in English, in which he was acquiring some proficiency.

⁂

Agnes Elisabeth Winona Leclerq Joy had a mysterious background that she never made any attempt to clarify. She was the daughter of William Joy, a descendant of Thomas Joy who came to Boston from England in the middle of the seventeenth century. She was born in 1840 (or possibly in 1844) in Philipsburg, Quebec, at the northern end of Lake Champlain, practically on the border with Vermont. She gave the date as 28 December, which was also Felix's birth-date. A story circulated later, one of several, that the invalid wife of an American cabinet minister, charmed by her ways, had picked her up in Paris and brought her to the US. The minister is never named, and the story is certainly suspect, but it added to the mystique. Another version had her born in Baltimore, daughter of a French-Canadian professional soldier.

As a *New York Herald* article noted years later, 'She was silent when questioned about her birth and never refuted any story that came to her ears'.[1] Indeed, she derived considerable amusement from all the speculation. She confessed at one point that it even offered her 'a malicious pleasure to disappoint a number of persons who have taken the trouble of inventing the most romantic and wonderful stories in reference to my youth'.

The descendants of the original Thomas Joy gradually spread westward, but the line that led to Agnes settled in northern New England, most particularly in small towns in northern Vermont near the Quebec border. They were farmers, carpenters, small merchants. About 1846, William, Agnes's father, moved across the border to Philipsburg.

Agnes said she was Catholic when she married Felix. This seems extraordinary for a Vermont girl of that era, but not for a Quebec girl. Perhaps William converted. If he did, there must have been a serious row with his family, and Agnes may have suffered the results. It is much more likely, however, that Agnes converted when she married Felix. Catholicism was a defining factor in his ancient family, and marriage to a Protestant was unthinkable. Agnes had probably a more laissez-faire attitude to religion, but the conversion may still have caused conflicts with her family.

The Joys were a prolific lot, by and large, and William had five children by his first wife and eight, including Agnes, by his second. With the exception of her younger sister Delia, with whom and with whose husband Agnes was very close, she never mentions any other member of her family, including her father, who lived on in Philipsburg until about 1866, and her mother. This certainly indicates some profound alienation, or perhaps she just found them boring. Her small-town childhood was probably hard and unrewarding, and she may as a girl have gone into domestic service in nearby Swanton, Vermont. For a girl of Agnes's temperament, that must have been hard indeed.

From an early age she was mad about horses, and in time became an accomplished horsewoman. One can imagine young

Agnes galloping across country, hair flying, thrilling in the escape her horse provided from the humdrum realities of her daily chores. Plodding little girls do not take up riding. In later years, she preferred to ride astride rather than sidesaddle, a habit that caused either amusement or scandal, depending.

While still in her early teens, it is said, she ran away from home and joined one of the many small itinerant circuses that roamed around the country, setting up for a night or two and then moving on. She must have met a grand cast of characters – the bearded lady, the sword-swallower, the magician, the contortionist, the acrobats and all the denizens of a world quite beyond anything she had known. It cannot have been common for teenaged girls in mid-nineteenth-century Vermont to run away to circuses, and the fact that Agnes did so says a lot about her rebellious, adventuresome spirit.

She never returned home. She put her childhood behind her, and along with it most of her family. They had nothing to offer her and she dropped them. Only her sister Delia played any role in her life.

She tried her hand at the high wire, and when the circus was in Chicago in the spring of 1858 she made her first public appearance as 'Agnes Leclerq, the Great Ascensionist'. Leclerq was apparently a name from her mother's family, and Agnes must have thought it had a more theatrical ring than 'Joy'. It was a very windy day and she fell, fortunately into the arms of a waiting acrobat who had taken the precaution of standing beneath her. Nothing daunted, she was back up on the wire within moments, and completed her walk to wild applause which must have whetted her developing sense of the theatrical. Many years later, in a press interview, Agnes denied the story of the high-wire act, but by that time it had become firmly embedded in the Agnes legend.

The circus toured the Mid-West, but then, as was often the case with these precarious operations, went bankrupt or fell foul of the sheriff, or both. Details are lacking, but in any case it closed. Perhaps with the aid of some of her circus friends, Agnes then made her way to Havana, where she worked at various jobs, including, apparently, in a nightclub. She wrote that she was in Cuba 'for several years'. This sojourn gave rise to yet another story about her origins: that she was the daughter of a French planter in Cuba. It was from Havana in 1861 that she came to New York to visit her sister prior to going to Washington and the McClellan parades and a much wider stage than she had played on heretofore.

Most of what we know of Agnes is from her own account, and that did not begin until 1862 when she burst fully armoured as the Princess Salm-Salm on the Washington scene. The few remarks in the family history by her cousin James Joy are not particularly illuminating, and one is left in the dark about many things. Nowhere, for one important example, is there any indication of what sort of an education she received, nor when nor where she received it. Yet she suddenly emerged from the shadows when she met Felix as an articulate, apparently reasonably well-educated young woman who proved able to hold her own, and then some, with the movers and shakers of society. The fact is that Agnes's life before she met Felix can be seen only fitfully, and for whatever reason she never saw fit to enlighten anyone. Contemporaries writing about her, and later writers as well, simply repeat whichever of the stories about her origin appealed to them, and rely on her book for details.

There is no disagreement from any source about her beauty and vivacity. She was a whirlwind of energy, impulsive and daring. Noah Brooks, a newspaperman and intimate friend of President Lincoln who knew Agnes in Washington, was one of the many men beguiled by her. 'She claimed American parentage,' he wrote,

> but was Italian in personal appearance, French in manner and spirit, and decidedly Bohemian in her tastes. When in the prime of womanhood she was a very beautiful person, and as charming as beautiful. Her face was oval, with regular, but unclassic features and profile, dark chestnut eyes, a delicate and finely-molded chin and mouth, dark wavy hair, and a singularly brilliant and winsome smile. In brief, she was a fascinating little woman, perfectly bewitching where she determined to bewitch, and never sullen, grave, or morose to any body. Sunny and gay as the Italy of our youthful romance, she was often more like a sprite than a woman of flesh and blood.[2]

She was also a very determined and absolutely fearless woman. When Agnes wanted something, she had no truck with underlings but went straight to the top. Her audacity, wrote Brooks, was 'simply consummate'. And the top – the President, state governors, cabinet members, generals – was amazingly accessible in those days. It was all part of the American brand of democracy – open, unpretentious, unencumbered by ceremony and the worship of tradition. Americans felt that even the White House was theirs to visit at pleasure, and many sources describe how easy it was to gain access and the shambles of receptions when the curious snipped pieces from the curtains and the upholstery. It was also a highly political society, with military commands going to men with political influence or connections. And the ambitious could easily find the right connections.

Despite the concern in government circles and the existence of war at the gates, Washington was gay with revelry. Noah Brooks again:

> The hotels were crowded with epauleted and shoulderstrapped officers of the army and navy; contractors spent money like water; Congressmen were badgered and hunted by anxious sharp men and women, who had plenty of money to use for certain purposes; the lobbies of the National Capitol swarmed with rapacious place-hunters and professional jobbers; vast sums were squandered daily for military supplies, and army commissions were dealt out like cheap trifles – rewards for the mere asking. In this exciting hurly-burly, Agnes was having a happy time. She loved the military better than the circus; brass buttons were dearer to her soul than spangles, and gold lace and silver stars more charming than the gay velvets and muslin banners of the sawdust ring. She felt that her destiny had come at last.[3]

Agnes was not alone in her enthusiasm. The ladies of Washington were known for their fondness for the military garb, for parades and for the dashing young officers who poured into town from all over the Union.

She often affected military garb, and when she appeared on Pennsylvania Avenue she was a sight to behold. Her riding habit was bedecked with gold buttons and braid, not to mention a captain's stripe. A mounted groom in livery followed behind. Noah Brooks described the splendid appearance of this 'dashing and fascinating beauty who had the hearts of half the men in

Washington, and the bitter hatred and ill-will of nearly every woman in that thronged city'.

⁂

There was no mystery, on the other hand, about Felix. Prince Felix Constantin Alexander Johann Nepomuk zu Salm-Salm was born at Anholt, in the Rhine province of Prussia, on 28 December 1828, the third and youngest son of Florentin, ninth Prince Salm and fourth Prince Salm-Salm. The Salms were an ancient family of the Rhineland that in the course of centuries had split into several princely branches of which Salm-Salm was the eldest. Anholt, where the ancestral *Schloss* still stands, is just north of the Rhine where that river crosses the border from Germany into the Netherlands.

The Salms were staunch Catholics and had served the emperors of the Habsburg line for centuries. Count Niklas von Salm-Reifferscheidt gained fame by his heroic defence of Vienna against the armies of Sultan Sulayman the Magnificent in 1529, and there were other noted Salms in the Church, the army and even science.

A cloud first appeared in 1614 when the Protestant Hohenzollern rulers of Brandenburg, ancestors of the kings (as they became in 1701) of Prussia, acquired the duchy of Cleves, across the Rhine from Anholt, after a five-year inheritance controversy that involved most of the European powers, including England. Prussian influence grew steadily stronger in northern Germany. Then came the tornado unleashed by Napoleon.

In the course of the Napoleonic Wars, the Salm lands on the west bank of the Rhine were lost to France, as were those of other princes. The peace settlements of 1815 awarded the west bank to Prussia, plus territory on the east bank, from which was created Prussia's Rhine province, with its capital at Coblenz. For three fleeting years (1803–6) in those chaotic times, Prince Constantin, Felix's grandfather, actually ruled a small Salm principality made up of Anholt and adjacent territories he was awarded in compensation for his losses, but in the end that too went to Prussia.

In the heady days of the Holy Roman Empire, the Salms and another hundred or so princely families with sovereign rights had the privilege of being *Reichsunmittelbar*, meaning that they stood directly below the emperor with no intervening feudal authority. In the tortuous and painful negotiations that followed the abolition of the empire in 1806 and the regulation of the status of the crowd of formerly sovereign German princes, the Salms and their fellows were 'mediatised'. This meant that they were placed under the jurisdiction of other sovereigns, the kings of Prussia in the case of the Salms. They did, however, preserve the important privilege of equality of birth that enabled them to marry into royalty on equal terms. The Salms therefore sat at the very pinnacle of German society. This tangled history also explains how the Salms could serve both their Protestant over-lords of Prussia and the Catholic Habsburg emperors of Austria with such perfect equanimity.

Young Felix joined the Prussian army, and in 1846 was gazetted a second lieutenant, being assigned the following year to the 11th Hussar Regiment. About this time the very compli-cated problem of the duchies of Schleswig and Holstein, a long-standing source of friction between Denmark and Prussia, came to one of its periodic boils, and Prussia sent an army into the duchies. The Prussians drove through the duchies into Danish territory, and on 28 May 1849 attacked the town of Århus. With more zeal than good sense, Felix persuaded a troop of hussars to follow him against a superior enemy force, and was sorely wounded by a sword slash and taken prisoner.

This was his first engagement, and it earned him a com-mendation from the future King Wilhelm I of Prussia, who sent him a sword of honour engraved 'Für Tapferkeit' ('for bravery').

His father, who had indulged him outrageously, died in 1846, and his eldest brother Prince Alfred became head of the clan. Alfred, who had a growing family, was considerably less indulgent toward his youngest brother, who, in addition to running up sizeable debts, acquired an expensive mistress, a very handsome Viennese actress. Between the debts and the actress, Felix was persuaded to resign from Prussian service – against the advice of friends and mentors – and go to Vienna to enter Austrian service. This in itself was not unusual for a Salm, of course, but in Felix's case the circumstances were neither particularly honourable nor voluntary. The change of scene apparently removed all restraints, and the young man was soon squarely in the clutches of moneylenders as his debts grew out of bounds.

It seems that a wealthy Jewish banker offered to settle Felix's debts if he would make his daughter a princess. She was an attractive and accomplished young lady, and Felix was agreeable to the idea, but then he wrecked the plan by showing up with his mistress at the opera in a box opposite that of the banker and his daughter. They were both deeply offended, and the match was off. The reaction of the Salm family to all this can be imagined. With his debts unresolved, Felix decamped for Paris.

A slightly jaundiced view of Salm is provided by a future comrade in arms in America, Baron Friedrich Otto von Fritsch. In his memoirs, Fritsch wrote,

> Felix Prince Salm-Salm had received a liberal education, and was one of the most high-toned and cavalier-like persons in Europe, but he was wonderfully extravagant. His generous private income as a Lieutenant in the Cavalry was soon squandered, and he contracted many debts. His wealthy brother paid these for him several times, but finally withdrew his assistance, and, pressed by creditors, the Prince was obliged to tender his resignation just when the war broke out in the States. To get rid of him, his brother bought him a passage over and advanced him a few hundred dollars in New York.[4]

Fritsch was not fond of Felix, and his remarks probably were prejudiced, but he provides balance to Agnes's almost always sunny picture.

At the beginning of his book on his experiences in Mexico, Felix wrote that he 'was a soldier with all my soul and war was my element'. The outbreak of the Civil War in the US thus offered him a chance to do what he liked best, and of course to escape from his creditors.

He arrived in the US in the late summer of 1861, armed, as was customary in those days, with letters of introduction. For starters he had one from the Prussian crown prince to the Prussian minister in Washington, Baron von Gerolt. Gerolt, who was Prussian minister for an astonishing 25 years (1846–71), was a close friend of President Lincoln. The *New York Herald* of 14 September 1861 reported the prince's arrival and his presentation to Secretary of State William Seward by Gerolt. The article made much of his military experience, stretching the truth not a little, and applauded his offer to serve the Union. That a man of his qualifications, recommended by his government, should step forward was, said the writer, 'a good omen'.

In any case, Gerolt took Felix around to see the President in the hope of securing him an appointment. Gerolt spoke glowingly of Felix's military experience, and then mentioned that he was a prince of highest rank. Accounts of the interview vary, but Lincoln apparently clapped Felix on the back and said 'That won't hurt you with us,' or words to that effect.

The President asked Secretary of War Simon Cameron to see if he could fix Felix up with a cavalry regiment. Cameron, in turn, wrote to the governor of Pennsylvania, who replied that he would be happy to oblige if another regiment of cavalry was authorised. This apparently did not happen because about the same time Felix was attached as Colonel of Cavalry to Louis Blenker's division. Agnes suggests that the prospect of a cavalry command when he spoke no English panicked Felix, and a post with Blenker in a comfortably German environment was more practical. Blenker appointed him Chief of Staff. It was at this point that he and Agnes met.

Blenker's division was known to be something of a waiting-room for immigrant German officers seeking a regular appointment. But beyond this select crew, the German element in the Union army was both formidable and important.

2

The Germans and Ludwig Blenker

Germans constituted the largest element of the immigrant population of the northern states in the early nineteenth century. They were hard-working and reliable, and as the great debate heated up were generally found on the anti-slavery side. To this base of solid but politically rather apathetic citizens was added a significant number of statesmen and soldiers who fled Germany after the failure of the liberal revolutions of 1848–49. Germany had been swept by revolutionary fervour inspired by the 1848 revolution in France that had ousted King Louis Philippe. These émigrés had fought for their liberties against autocratic monarchs, and they stood squarely on the side of liberty, freedom and equality.

President Lincoln had already identified himself with German interests. As a rising politician in Illinois, he had recognised the importance of gaining immigrant support, and he was responsible for measures that granted equality of rights to the foreign born. His campaign for the US Senate in 1858 was unsuccessful, but he spoke out strongly against slavery and drew the German vote. The '48ers' led the way. By the hundreds they joined Lincoln's Republican Party. With their help Lincoln secured the Republican nomination for president in 1860. Later, as president, he spoke of the need to encourage immigration to boost the sparse population of the US.

When in 1861 Lincoln called for volunteers, the Germans flocked to the Union colours. The American legation in Berlin was so flooded with offers to volunteer that it had to put out special bulletins that it was not a recruiting office. Germany provided war material and money. Lincoln's friend Gerolt, the Prussian minister, was solidly pro-Union, and reported favourably on the Union cause to his government.

There was also a serious shortage of competent American officers, as the opening months of the war would demonstrate all too clearly. The West Point Military Academy had been founded in 1802 and had turned out some good men, but their practical experience in fighting had been pretty much limited to Indians and Mexicans. There were not enough trained officers for the job ahead – on either side.

The state governors, who were required to produce their quotas of volunteer regiments, often appointed colonels not because of their military records but because of their political influence or ability to recruit. The procedure for an ambitious man was first to secure a colonelcy and then to recruit a regiment. The advantages of political clout were well displayed in the advancement of Felix zu Salm-Salm, as we will see.

German officers played an important role in the Union army. Three, all 48ers, rose to the rank of major general: Franz Sigel, Carl Schurz and Peter Joseph Osterhaus. Of the ten who became brigadier generals, five were 48ers, including Louis Blenker. Others had come in the 1840s and had served in the Mexican war. There were also many colonels and lesser ranks of German background. These men were not only convinced democrats, but could boast of active service with infantry, cavalry and artillery commands. They possessed desperately needed skills that were in very short supply in the US. Blenker was to give Felix his first chance. He was by all accounts a considerable character.

Ludwig Blenker (1812–63) was born in Worms in the grand duchy of Hesse. He enlisted as a private in the Bavarian Legion raised in 1833 to escort Otto von Wittelsbach, the Bavarian prince whom the Great Powers had chosen to be king of newly independent Greece. He returned to Germany after six years, having achieved the rank of lieutenant, and took up medical studies. A decade later he was caught up in the liberal movements that swept Germany and became a member of the revolutionary government in Baden formed after the grand duke fled in 1849. He was also made commander of the national guard. When the revolution was crushed by Prussian troops, Blenker fled first to Switzerland and then to the US, where he settled into business in New York City. He also purchased a farm in Rockland County, not far from the city.

At the outbreak of the Civil War, Blenker, with his military background, had no trouble securing a colonelcy. With the aid of Lt Colonel Julius Stahel, a Hungarian who had also fought in the 1848–49 rebellions, he raised the 8th New York Infantry Volunteers (the '1st German Rifles'), mustered in by the end of April for a two-year term. This was in time to be Felix's regiment.

Blenker was famous for his flair and theatricality. He wore a great red-lined cloak, entertained lavishly and lived well, but he also saw to it that his men were properly outfitted and cared for, something of a rarity in those days. The 1st German Rifles not only had a full complement of a thousand men, it had an artillery unit and a medical detachment, the men had both regular and dress uniforms, and there were special squads of sappers and miners. The regiment made a great impression when it marched down Broadway on 26 May 1861 and embarked for Washington.

By the summer of 1861, Blenker's reputation had gained him command of a brigade in the Army of Northeast Virginia, while Julius Stahel took over command of the 8th New York Volunteers. As we have seen, Blenker's Brigade was held in reserve in the rear at the First Battle of Bull Run on 21 July, and was widely credited with having prevented the Confederates from reaching Washington. He was made brigadier general on 9 August 1861, and Blenker's Division was organised. Its three brigades and the 12 regiments that in total composed them were all commanded by Germans, except for two regiments commanded by a Hungarian and a Pole, also 48ers.

In November 1861 Blenker's Division moved across the Potomac to Hunter's Chapel, north of Alexandria. His headquarters there 'were the wonder and envy of the whole army of the Potomac,' wrote General Carl Schurz, another 48er who had done very well in his adopted country and had become a close friend of President Lincoln. Blenker's camp was laid out in orderly rows, with gardens and shrubs to soften the straight lines of tents. His own tent was lavishly appointed, and even General

McClellan came to visit and get the 'Blenker treatment'. But with all this, said Schurz, Blenker was a thoroughly brave man, an excellent organiser, and an efficient commander. His regiment was a model of good order, and the brigade he commanded at the First Battle of Bull Run stood firm, in perfect order, as the rout tumbled by.

Another German chronicler of these events, Wilhelm Kaufmann, wrote,

> Blenker, the old democrat, had a remarkable partiality for noble officers. Around him swarmed counts, lords and barons, and even a German prince [Salm-Salm] was there. Blenker's 'casino of nobles' was much ridiculed in the contemporary press. The Forty-Eighters were particularly indignant and an antagonism developed between the officers from the ranks of former German revolutionaries and Blenker's company of nobles.[5]

The democratic sentiments of the 48ers were outraged by Blenker's exhibitionism and by the German aristocrats, most of them soldiers of fortune with scant democratic credentials, who attached themselves to his command. He came under bitter attack from several German-American newspapers, and was accused of financial finagling, tolerating his soldiers' looting of Virginia farms and encouraging dissolute behaviour. His lavish lifestyle seemed beyond the salary of a colonel, but nothing was ever proved against him.

Blenker seemed able to procure limitless supplies of beer for his men, which made his camp an attractive target for those who belonged to less exotic commands. They had to face a prevailing odour of sauerkraut, but that could be managed. He also secured the privilege of selling beer, reported Kaufmann, so his camp at Hunter's Chapel 'soon became the focus of a pilgrimage for soldiers from other divisions, and the consumption of beer in the German camp at times reminded one of the Munich Oktoberfest'.[6]

General McClellan was not immune to the Blenker treatment. In his memoirs, the general described the scene:

> The most entertaining part of my duties were those which sometimes led me to Blenker's camp…As soon as we were sighted, Blenker would have the 'officer's call' blown to

assemble his polyglot collection, with their uniforms as varied and brilliant as the colors of the rainbow. Wrapped in his scarlet-lined cloak, his group of officers ranged around him, he would receive us with the most formal and polished courtesy. Being a very handsome and soldierly-looking man himself, and there being many equally so among his surroundings, the tableau was always very effective, and presented a striking contrast to the matter-of-fact way in which things were managed in the other divisions. In a few minutes he would shout, 'Ordinanz numero eins!' whereupon champagne would be brought in great profusion, the bands would play, sometimes songs be sung.[7]

Felix became attached to Blenker's staff on 17 September 1861 with the rank of colonel, and seems at the same time to have served in the District of Columbia Militia raised for three months to guard the capital, not a riveting assignment for him. When Blenker's Division was moved to Virginia in November, Felix was often seen in Washington. The dashing young aristocrat made the best of the swirling social life. He was spotted among the guests who attended the famous White House ball in February 1862. Mary Todd Lincoln, a compulsive spender, lavished so much money on the ball that the President despaired. It was the most extravagant social event of the new – and wartime – presidency and caused great offence to many. Mary Lincoln had issued 500 invitations for the party, when the tradition was that White House receptions (as opposed to dinners) were open to all.

These pastimes were soon put aside. To the growing annoyance of the President and the administration, who wanted swift and decisive action, McClellan had spent months preparing the Army of the Potomac for an attack on Richmond, capital of the Confederacy. He proposed to transport the army to the mouth of the James River and advance up the peninsula to his goal. Just as he was about to get under way, the President ordered Blenker's Division to join General John C. Frémont's Mountain Division in the Shenandoah Valley in western Virginia.

There was a real fear in Washington that the redoubtable Confederate General Thomas 'Stonewall' Jackson would swoop down the Shenandoah Valley and strike at the capital, and it was considered essential that Frémont be reinforced. McClellan was furious at losing Blenker, and he and the President exchanged sharp telegrams, but on 6 April Blenker's Division set off.

They promptly ran into heavy snow alternating with drenching rain. Even under optimal conditions it would have been a tough haul through rough roadless country over the Blue Ridge Mountains and swollen creeks and rivers to Petersburg, Virginia, Frémont's headquarters. But there was more. Through some incredible muddle, the War Department seems to have forgotten all about them. The division lacked the most basic equipment, from tents to coats to shoes, not to mention forage, provisions and horses. They did not even have proper maps. The men suffered dreadful hardships. Blenker was injured in a fall from his horse, and the insufficient rations drove the men to raid farms along the route. The unfortunate Germans staggered cross-country in the cold rain, shedding their sick and stragglers en route. When an improvised ferry sank crossing the Shenandoah River, 20 officers and men were lost.

When the War Department finally realised that it had lost a division, it sent General William S. Rosecrans to find it. The hunt took several days. Rosecrans was shocked by what he found. He reported to Secretary of War Stanton that the men were short of virtually everything they should have had for their own provisioning and maintenance and that of their horses. It was no wonder that they stole liberally from the farms along the way.

Rosecrans did what he could to reprovision them, and rushed them to Frémont at Petersburg, where they arrived on 11 May. Fewer than 6000 of Blenker's original force of 10,000 were present for duty. The remainder had disappeared, drowned or were too badly off to fight. With little time for the exhausted and demoralised men to rest, Frémont set out in pursuit of Jackson. He found him at Cross Keys on 7 June, but the wily Southerner outwitted and defeated him on 8 June. In the course of the battle, Blenker's Division was repulsed with heavy losses in an attempt to turn the Confederate left flank.

Blenker was not to blame for the debacle, but tongues wagged and he was again accused of financial irregularities. Nothing was ever proven, but he was relieved of his command (to be succeeded by Franz Sigel, another refugee from the 1848 revolution in Baden) and called back to Washington. He saw no more action, and was discharged from the army on 31 March 1863. He returned to his farm in Rockland County, where he died on 31 October of the same year from injuries sustained in the fall from his horse the previous spring. It was a sad end for the old freedom fighter; he was only 51.

Frémont was also relieved of his command. Sigel was promoted to replace him. The Germans were very proud of him, and the cry 'I fights mit Sigel' became a byword. Sigel's command was ultimately designated the XI Corps of the Army of the Potomac and was perceived throughout the army as a German command. Only 15 of its 26 regiments were German, but it was the Germans who set the tone.

How Felix managed through all this is unknown, but his personnel files locate him in the Shenandoah Valley at the right times, so he must have participated in the march, and he is reported to have been at Cross Keys. An entry of 29 June indicates that he was on furlough from his post as Chief of Staff in Stahel's Brigade, 2nd Division. On 30 August 1862, as we have seen, he was married to Agnes in Washington.

Agnes was not particularly interested in military matters at the time, and says nothing about the hardships endured by her betrothed. She was much more concerned with the social life and the influential figures among whom she now moved and with whom she connived for her husband's advancement. She also started to become involved with hospital work, in which she showed a genius for organisation and a capacity for effective hard work to alleviate some of the miseries of the sick and wounded.

But there was work to be done, and quickly. Blenker's virtual disgrace after Cross Keys and his removal from command meant the end of his lavish personal staff of aristocratic aides, the chief of whom was Prince Felix zu Salm-Salm.

3

The 8th New York Volunteers

So far, Felix's career in the Union army had not been in any way remarkable. It was time for the newly minted Princess Salm-Salm to remedy that state of affairs.

Edwin Stanton had been made Secretary of War in January 1862. He was an implacable foe of corruption, crooked contractors and procrastinating generals. Favour-seekers were given short shrift. He whipped the War Department into shape and kept the armies in the field moving and well supplied (with the notable exception of the unfortunate Blenker).

He had little time for bloated staffs such as Blenker's, and in the early autumn of 1862 Agnes learned that he had dismissed several of them and had his eye on Felix. Prompt action was required. 'The only step that could save him,' she wrote, 'was to procure at once the command of a regiment in the field from some governor before this official notice was given, and for this purpose we started directly for New York.'

Agnes had by now spent almost a year in Washington, where she had been an assiduous observer and learner. She quickly realised that if she and Felix were to prosper, they needed the help of influential friends. This was the way of Washington. With Felix in the field, Agnes had the opportunity to focus on those most likely to assist them. Congress was in session, and cabinet ministers were all about. 'Congress, and especially the Senate, was the spring of grace, and whoever had friends in that august body was sure of success,' she observed astutely.

The ladies of the capital were expert wheelers and dealers who sought to gain favours for their husbands and friends. Lucrative opportunities abounded in the military and civilian contracting business and in the military itself. 'Washington was then reputed as a most wicked and dissipated place,' Agnes wrote, 'and ladies that could not afford to pay it a visit shuddered at its wickedness, whilst it was the highest desire of all the rest, especially if good-looking, to pass a season in this abominable place.'

There was Agnes, through and through. She learned to play the game expertly.

The ladies of the capital also received mention from Margaret Leech in her book *Reveille in Washington*:

> [Washington] was a society which permitted an unusual free-dom to ladies. Moving breathlessly and without privacy in a shower of white kid gloves and calling cards, they had a role to play in the parlors; and might still enjoy homage at an age when in other American cities they would have been relegated to knitting by the fireside. The galleries of the 'sacred' Capitol were bright with their bonnets. They thronged its corridors, sending in their cards to summon acquaintances from the floor of the Senate and House.[8]

Among Agnes's new friends was Senator Ira Harris of New York, who just happened to be a close counsellor of President Lincoln and who wielded considerable power as a member of the Judiciary and Foreign Relations Committees. He was at the time in Albany. In view of the news from the War Department, the Salms decided to hurry to the upstate New York capital to see if they could persuade him to arrange an audience with Governor Edwin D. Morgan, who might have a spare regiment that needed a colonel.

Morgan had done fine work in helping raise New York State's quota of 17 regiments when Lincoln had first called for volunteers, and a number of these were composed of Germans. Lincoln had commissioned Morgan a Brigadier General of Volunteers in September 1861, as well as commander of the New York Military District. Before he completed his term of office in 1862, he had helped raise and equip 120 regiments. He was an ideal target for Agnes.

Agnes went to see Senator Harris alone. Felix still spoke insufficient English, and she felt it prudent that he remain in the background for the moment. The senator was not sanguine – the governor was a tough customer who did not succumb easily to blandishments – but in the end he agreed to go with Agnes and introduce her to Morgan. This was to be her first big test.

She and Harris were admitted to Morgan's office, where he fixed them with a 'calm, stern eye'.

> With a faltering voice I commenced pleading for my husband. I spoke of his ardent desire to serve the cause of the Republic, and described his despair at being kept inactive when his comrades won honour in the field. I praised his military qualities, and dwelt on the proofs which he had given me of them. I became warmer and warmer. I spoke for about a quarter of an hour, and he never helped me with a word.

But in the end, he thawed.

There were indeed several regiments available, but they were mostly American. Nervous about Felix's English, she asked if he could be given command of one of the German regiments. Yes, there was one free – the 8th New York.

Agnes was thrilled, but she had to push for one more favour. She asked that the commission be made out and signed at once, fearing that if the news came out that Felix was due for dismissal, he might lose this new chance. The Governor seems to have been charmed, or bemused, by Agnes. He had the commission written up and signed it on the spot. Agnes rushed back to the hotel where she and Felix celebrated this happy turn of events. They returned to Washington, and at the end of October 1862 Felix took command of the 8th New York Volunteer Regiment at Aldie, in northern Virginia.

The encounter with Governor Morgan was the first real test of Agnes's powers of persuasion. It was not enough to know the right people to approach to get what she wanted. They had to be convinced, and Agnes had an extraordinary talent for convincing. She was to perfect this ability in the years to come, with ever greater effect.

This again raises the question of Agnes's education. No unlettered country bumpkin or circus performer could possibly have made the impact she did on important political figures. She had to have had the language and the manners to persuade them to go along with her.

⁂

This was the same 8th New York Regiment raised by Blenker and Stahel in April 1861. Stahel had taken over command in June when Blenker moved up to brigade level. The 8th had seen serious action in the war and had suffered heavy losses, including those at Cross Keys in the Shenandoah Valley on 8 June 1862.

There was thus some murmuring of discontent when this relatively unseasoned prince took over the command. Captain Gustav von Struve, a radical revolutionary from Baden, was outraged at the appointment of Felix and resigned his post, proclaiming that he could not be a servant of princes. He returned to Germany, embittered.

Unfortunately, though indeed he had his command, Felix saw little real action. There were reconnaissance expeditions, there were excursions and alarms, but not much that a brave and energetic officer could get his teeth into despite the action that swirled around him. The Confederates had won a second victory at Bull Run on 30 August, the day Agnes and Felix were wed, and immediately afterward General Robert E. Lee crossed the Potomac into Maryland. The ferocious battle at Antietam on 17 September left a total of 20,000 dead on the field. It was indecisive, but Lee did pull back into Virginia.

The way to Richmond, the Confederate capital in Virginia, lay open, but despite the orders of his government to advance, McClellan stood pat for some six weeks before starting south. The delay allowed Lee to regroup, and he suddenly moved to place his army between McClellan and Richmond. This was the final blow for the Union commander. McClellan had never made any pretence of his disdain for the President, or Secretary of War Stanton, or General-in-Chief Henry W. Halleck. He was convinced of his own superiority. On 7 November 1862 he was replaced as commander of the Army of the Potomac by General Ambrose E. Burnside.

As soon as she could, Agnes arranged to follow Felix to Aldie. She was escorted on this occasion by Colonel Otto von Corvin. Corvin (1812–86) had also taken part in the 1848 rebellion in Baden, had been captured and condemned to death. He was spared, however, and after serving a prison sentence went to London. He had come to the US in 1861 as a correspondent for *The Times* of London and the *Augusburger Allgemeine Zeitung.* He of course knew Blenker, through whom Felix met him. Corvin and his wife became close friends of the Salms and were at their wedding. In 1867 he returned to Germany as a correspondent for the *New York Times*, for which he covered the Franco–Prussian War.

In a book written ten years later, Corvin made several illuminating remarks about the Salms. He and his wife grew very fond of the young couple, but Corvin was not uncritical. 'I liked him,' he wrote, 'for he was extremely modest and unpretending, and one of the best-natured, kindest-hearted men I ever met. He had no brilliant talents, and no strength of character, and he felt in America like a fish out of water.'[9] Accustomed to a cosseted aristocratic upbringing in the Old World, Felix often found the rough-and-ready society of America offensive, and he had difficulty fitting in. Then, too, the democratic German press in New York behaved 'shamefully' to him. As a prince he was their natural enemy. Corvin, whose democratic credentials were unassailable, stood up for Felix against his detractors, and the younger man was deeply grateful.

As a good-looking prince, Corvin observed, Felix could have had his pick of wealthy American girls, but he fell 'vehemently in love' with Agnes, a very pretty lady but without wealth or background. Corvin noted that the Salm family history was dotted with hot-blooded members entering into *mésalliances*, and he cautioned Felix against the marriage. But Felix insisted, and Corvin finally agreed to be a witness at the marriage ceremony, which was performed by a Catholic priest in his chambers near St Patrick's Church in Washington, not in the church, as Agnes maintained.

Baron von Gerolt chided Corvin for having encouraged the marriage, another indication of aristocratic Prussian prejudice, but the deed was done.

When Mrs Corvin joined her husband, Agnes took to her at once, as Felix had to Corvin, and the two couples remained friends for years, sharing lodgings and adventures.

Returning to Aldie, the night after Agnes arrived word came that the enemy was advancing, and the Union forces retired to Chantilly, some dozen miles to the east. Agnes and Corvin rode ahead in a drizzling rain that soon turned worse. The ride was 'no pleasure party,' wrote Agnes, but she persuaded Corvin to carry under his rain gear 'a large and fine red ostrich plume for my hat, which I did not want to have spoiled'. The weather continued terrible, and when orders came for the XI Corps to march south to Falmouth, just northeast of Fredericksburg on the Rappahannock River, Felix prevailed upon Agnes to return to Washington until such time as the troops reached winter quarters.

The corps moved out on 10 December, and was still on the march when Burnside and Lee met at Fredericksburg on 13 December. It was another Union disaster. To redeem himself, Burnside decided to march the army several miles up the Rappahannock, cross over and fall on the Confederate rear. They moved out on 19 January 1863. The weather was appalling, with torrential rain and high winds that persisted for 48 hours. Men, horses, guns – everything – bogged down in the mud and in the end Burnside had to give up. He was relieved of his command on 25 January, to be succeeded by General Joseph Hooker. Felix seems to have missed this debacle as well, because he and Agnes celebrated their birthdays on 28 December 1862 in winter quarters at Stafford, near the Potomac, some 10 miles north of Fredericksburg. He had sent for her to join him, and she came down from Washington on a gunboat.

The 8th New York was camped in a pine grove, on the slope of a hill not far from the divisional headquarters of its former commander, Stahel, who had been promoted to brigadier general in November 1861. The soldiers had laid out a garden, with flower beds outlined in stones, and had planted shrubs and trees. They had also created an enormous 'birthday cake' of mud, ornamented with green leaves, coloured sand, and stones representing fruit. Stahel sent a band to serenade the couple on the morning of the twenty-eighth. It was all very *gemütlich*.

When the officers came to congratulate us, we wished of course to offer them some refreshment; and with the utmost difficulty Salm procured four bottles of very vile whiskey, for which he had to pay eight dollars a bottle. Sugar and some lemons were procured also, and we could treat our guests with a punch which found immense favour with them, though it was a most abominable, abundantly watered stuff. We were, however, as merry and happy as could be.

The party of the season was that given on New Year's Eve 1862 by General Daniel E. Sickles. Sickles had gained considerable notoriety as a congressman before the war by shooting his wife's lover, the son of Francis Scott Key, composer of 'The Star-Spangled Banner'. For this sumptuous occasion, he had put together several hospital tents that were decorated with flags, garlands, flowers and Chinese lanterns. 'The supper,' she wrote,

laid under the tent for about two hundred persons, ladies and gentlemen, could not have been better in Paris, for the famous Delmonico from New York had come himself to superintend the repast, and brought with him his kitchen aides and batteries, and immense quantities of the choicest provisions and delicacies, together with plate and silver, and whatever was required to make one forget that it was a camp supper. The wines and liquors were in correspondence with the rest, and no less, I suppose, the bill to be paid.

In January 1863 the XI Corps was ordered to Aquia Creek, an important supply base and railhead on the Potomac downstream from Washington, east of Fredericksburg. The roads were beyond description, wrote Agnes. The mud was knee-deep and the troops had terrible difficulty moving the wagons and ordnance. Rumour had it that they were going to spend the winter there, and the Salms set out to make themselves as comfortable as possible.

Felix was determined to see that his bride of five months received the princely treatment he felt she deserved. He had found a large hospital tent, which was fixed up splendidly by the soldiers, who were in fact workmen of all trades: carpenters, furniture makers, upholsterers and the like. Carpets covered the floor and a fine sofa with comfortable cushions adorned the salon. Their bedroom had a commodious bed with a straw mattress, a blanket and a buffalo robe.

The crowning glory, wrote Agnes,

> was a large mirror which Salm, with great trouble, had pro-
> cured from a neighboring village, imagining that no lady
> could be happy without a looking-glass. I had, however, little
> need of it, as my toilet in the field was as simple as possible. I
> had a black and a grey riding dress – I must have a change, as
> we not rarely got drenched in our excursions on horseback –
> and two uniform-like costumes, which I adopted for the whole
> war-time in the field, consisting of a petticoat falling to my
> ankles, and a tight-fitting jacket, both of cloth.

Out back was a smaller tent for Agnes's servant girl and a shed
for the horses. Food was now in plentiful supply. 'We had our own
caterer, who provided us with all the delicacies of the season, and
our wine cellar, which was dug in the ground, contained bottles
of the most different shapes and contents.'

General Hooker permitted the families of both officers and
soldiers to visit and stay, and the place teemed with women and
children. The country was lovely, the weather had at last turned
fine, and the Salms were in high spirits. In the Army of the
Potomac she had found a true home, her first for a great many
years. Wrote Noah Brooks,

> Her love for the military and passion for horses were both
> gratified here as never before: wife of a staff officer, on fami-
> liar terms with hosts of Generals and Colonels, admired by
> all the army correspondents, and befriended by all the
> Washington politicians, she came and went with the army at
> her own sweet will.[10]

They were now joined by Captain von der Groeben, an old comrade of Felix from Germany, who assumed the role of major
domo. 'Old Groeben' was to be with Felix for the duration of
the war.

General Hooker spent the winter and spring preparing for
the upcoming campaign season. Spirits in the Union army began
to rise after the disasters of 1862. There was only one dark cloud
on the horizon, at least as far as the Salms were concerned. The
8th New York had been mustered in for two years, and this term
was up in April 1863. This had to be faced eventually, but in the
meantime life was to be enjoyed.

On 17 March 1863, the Irish Brigade, raised in New York and commanded by Thomas Francis Meagher, gave a very successful and rowdy party. The punch was said to have consisted of eight baskets of champagne, 10 gallons of rum and 22 gallons of Irish whisky, despite which there were steeplechases and various other sporting events to amuse the company.

Not to be outdone, General David Birney, 1st Division, III Corps, gave an answering blast on 27 March. Among those present was Colonel Charles S. Wainwright, 1st Regiment New York Volunteer Light Infantry, who left an account of the proceedings. A racecourse was built about a mile in the rear of army headquarters, and much of the action centred there. General officers, including Hooker, were present all day.

> How they managed to scare up such a number of females I cannot imagine. There must be a large number of officers' wives down there with the army now. Mrs Salm-Salm and Mrs Farnum, of course, were on hand. Both have been handsome women in their day, and are still good-looking enough to stand very well in the eyes of General Joe [Hooker]. The camps are full of stories about them both.
>
> The sports opened with flat and hurdle races, for officers riding their own horses. Some of the riding was quite good on the flat, but the horses shew that they were none of them much accustomed to jumping. Prince Salm-Salm was badly thrown, and so much injured that the first report was it would kill him. After the horseracing was over, there was foot and sack racing for the men, a greased pole to climb, and 'fighting cocks'. The last furnished the most amusement and was decidedly good. Two men are buckled, and then set on their feet when they try to butt each other over; their seconds setting them on their feet again whenever either one is upset. As a whole, the affair went off exceedingly well.[11]

Agnes's leading role in social events and her beauty and energy were grist for the local gossip mills. There was much talk and some slander, but Agnes sailed through it all unfazed. She was having too good a time. Besides, the clacking of jealous tongues notwithstanding, she and Felix were a good team, and they made a striking couple. His English seems to have improved considerably, which helped matters.

One other incident of their Aquia Creek stay is worth reporting. In April Hooker declared the army ready. The President and his family, Gerolt and others of the diplomatic corps, newspapermen including Noah Brooks, and assorted politicians came down to Aquia Creek for a grand review of the Army of the Potomac. Agnes made her mark – twice. Mrs Lincoln could not abide Agnes. She always called her 'Mrs Salm'. At one of the parades, Agnes and some of her friends appeared on horseback, and in the jostling for position managed to get ahead of Mrs Lincoln's carriage. You could not miss her. 'Mounted on a superb horse, and wearing a rich habit and a tall hat, from which floated a long, blue gauze veil, she cut a dashing figure everywhere.'[12] Mary Lincoln was livid, and demanded that Hooker get rid of all these women.

But more was to come. A review put on by General Sickles was followed by a reception and lunch. Stories vary, but it seems that Lincoln looked rather morose and Sickles encouraged the ladies to make the President feel welcome. Agnes promptly marched up to his table and gave him a hearty buzz on the cheek. He was startled, but took it good-naturedly, and other women followed suit. Mary Lincoln, jealous under ordinary circumstances, was fit to be tied when she learned of the incident.

Somewhat mischievously, knowing that Mrs Lincoln disliked Sickles, Hooker designated him to escort the presidential pair back to their steamboat at Aquia Creek. As supper was being served, in a rather tense atmosphere, Lincoln turned to Sickles and said he had never known until the previous evening that he was such a pious man. When the general protested that he was not, Lincoln said, 'Mother says you are the greatest psalmist in the army. She says you are more than a psalmist, you are a Salm-Salmist.'[13] Everyone burst into laughter, including Mary Lincoln, and peace was restored.

This merriment was short-lived. At the beginning of May, Hooker and Lee met at Chancellorsville, and in a battle over three days the Union forces were once again defeated. The Germans took heavy losses and it was a long time before their reputation recovered. Hooker was relieved of his command at his own request, and George C. Meade took over the Army of the Potomac, its fourth commander in two years.

Felix and the 8th New York were not present. The regiment's term of enlistment was up in April 1863 and most of the remaining men wanted out. They and the 7th New York came across the Potomac and marched across Washington to the railway depot accompanied by much cheering. Felix escorted them back to New York, where on 23 April they were mustered out, their colonel included. The three-year men were consolidated into a company, and in May were transferred to the 68th New York. At a lavish regimental party, Felix was presented with a sword of honour with a gold scabbard. Agnes gave in to calls for a speech. 'I had to comply, and my efforts to express myself in German were received with thunderous applause.' All very well, but Felix was out of a job again.

Agnes had, of course, been busy. Not content with a colonelcy, she wanted more for her husband. Witness the following dispatch, dated 30 March 1863 from Major General Daniel E. Sickles, III Corps, to the President:

Sir:

I have the honor to commend to the attention of Your Excellency the services of Prince Salm, of Prussia, a colonel in the Eighth New York Volunteers, with reference to his promotion. This distinguished officer has shared with us for more than a year the fortunes of our eventful war. He brought to our cause the experience of several campaigns in Europe and the professional advantages of a thorough military education. This is the first instance in which I have ventured to address a recommendation to the Government on behalf of any officer not serving in my own command, nor should I feel justified in this deviation from the rule hitherto prescribed for myself unless I had enjoyed the opportunity to assure myself of the eminent ability and worth of Colonel Salm. If he has not before been brought more directly to the notice of Your Excellency it is none the less flattering to his unobtrusive merit. And I am sure that it will be gratifying to the people of his country to see that the zeal and devotion of one who, following the illustrious example of La Fayette and Steuben [the Prussian general who reorganized George Washington's army in the Revolutionary War], has been signalized by that recognition which, fairly earned in the field and generously bestowed by those in authority, confers upon a soldier a recompense not more welcome than just. The regiment which Colonel Salm commands will be mustered out of service in the latter part of April. Unless promoted to the rank of brigadier-general, for which he is abundantly qualified, the service will lose in his unwilling retirement one of its most accomplished and faithful officers.[14]

This wordy, muddily written, dispatch, which inflated Felix's accomplishments considerably, was the first shot in Agnes's campaign to get a general's commission for her husband.

4

The 68th New York Volunteers

It was relatively easy to secure a new colonel's commission, but the War Department, not unreasonably, insisted that a colonel bring with him a regiment, or at least 700 men. Had the men of the 8th re-enlisted for another hitch, all would have been well, but most wanted to go home. Only about a hundred remained.

The Salms now took a house in New York, at 32 Bond Street, just east of Washington Square. This was their first proper residence. They plunged into the social whirl. 'No ball, reception or sword presentation was a success without their company,' noted the *New York Herald* some years later. 'He was the lion and she the belle of the hour.' During this period Agnes became friendly with James Gordon Bennett, founder and editor of the *New York Herald*. His son, James Gordon Bennett Jr, gave Agnes a little black and tan terrier pup she named 'Jimmy', who was to be her constant companion for many years ahead.

She also spent time in Washington, being 'very busy on behalf of my husband'. Horatio Seymour had by now succeeded Edwin Morgan, the Salms' earlier benefactor, as governor of New York State. He came through for the Salms, but his appointment of Felix as commander of the 68th New York Infantry Volunteers in June 1863 was distinctly a mixed blessing.

The 68th was another German regiment recruited in New York and mustered in on 1 August 1861. It was assigned initially to Blenker's Brigade, then to other commands, and saw a great deal of action in 1862 and 1863, including Gettysburg. Heavy losses had reduced the regiment to barely company strength, and in any case the term of enlistment for the original recruits was up in August.

The 68th was thus a tough, seasoned outfit. The purely political appointment of Prince Felix zu Salm-Salm as colonel commanding did not go down well. Several others felt they had a better claim. Among them was Baron Friedrich Otto von Fritsch, who came to the US in 1862 with the usual letters of recommendation to Gerolt. The Prussian minister declined to introduce him to President Lincoln because he had already asked so much of the president, but fortuitously Fritsch met the British minister, who took him along when he went to call at the White House. In the end, Fritsch was commissioned a first lieutenant in the 68th, saw action and was wounded at Chancellorsville (April 1863) and again at Gettysburg (July 1863). He left a memoir that casts interesting lights on life in the service and on the Salms.

The surviving men of the 68th returned to New York and marched up Broadway to resounding cheers, met the mayor and had a huge banquet. Fritsch was in command of Company A. He, Lt Colonel Albert von Steinhausen and most of the others wanted to re-enlist, but they objected to the rumoured appointment of Felix. Fritsch called on the banker August Belmont, also from Germany, to whom he had been recommended by the Rothschilds in Frankfurt. Belmont gave him a letter to Governor Seymour, but it was too late. Fritsch and Steinhausen went to Albany to protest the appointment of Felix, 'who had, before we reached New York, secured for himself the Colonecy of our regiment, in case we should re-enlist. His beautiful wife had done the talking – and a good deal of smiling and coaxing – as he had never learned to speak the English language fluently.'[15]

The 68th thus wound up with Felix as Colonel, Steinhausen as Lt Colonel and Fritsch as Senior Captain. While Felix remained in New York to recruit, the 68th under Steinhausen, somewhat strengthened by re-enlistees, returned to Virginia to rejoin the XI Corps of the Army of the Potomac under Hooker.

Felix opened a recruiting office at 619 Broadway, in Maillard's Hotel. But by now, the initial enthusiasm for volunteering had waned in the face of the awful losses in battle, the general incompetence of command and the hardships. The war was not going to end soon after all, and the supply of volunteers dried up. All manner of means were employed to attract men, but it was hard going.

And recruiting from abroad? Corvin, the Salms' correspondent friend, was all in favour of the idea. As he was close to Secretary of State William Seward, he and Felix went to Washington. Seward got them in to see Lincoln to lay out their plans for raising 20,000 men in Europe for the Union army. Lincoln was cautiously interested, though he recognised the problems with foreign governments that direct recruiting would doubtless cause, but Secretary of War Stanton was flatly opposed to the scheme. Corvin thought difficulties with foreign governments might be avoided if the President gave him and Felix authorisation simply to raise 20,000 troops; the choice of countries would be their responsibility and risk.

In the end, the scheme came to naught. There were too many potential complications with foreign governments, and Corvin undermined his case by hinting that he expected to make some money out of the plan.

Desperate for manpower, in March 1863 the government had passed the first conscription act. It was a flawed piece of legislation and fell most heavily on the poor: the wealthy could either furnish a substitute or pay $300 to get off. The first drawing of names in New York touched off appalling riots in which blacks were the chief sufferers. The Irish-American working class in New York had a history of anti-black prejudice, and what started off on the morning of Monday 13 July as a demonstration against the draft quickly expanded into a general assault on property, merchants and blacks. The German-American community, with many businesses and shops, organised in its own defence. Felix placed himself at the disposal of the city government, collected some troops from among his own recruits and others and led them against the rioters.

The municipal police were unable to regain control, and there were virtually no troops in the city. They had all been sent to Pennsylvania to check Lee's advance. The battle of Gettysburg was fought 1–3 July, and only after that bit of carnage could the

New York troops get back. They began arriving on Thursday the sixteenth and by the next day order had been restored.

Felix still needed men for the 68th, and was having a terrible time of it. Agnes marshalled her talents and went straight to the top. She turned again to their old friend Senator Ira Harris, who suggested she might call on the Provost-General in Washington, Colonel James B. Fry, who had men at his disposal. She arranged a meeting with Fry at once and made her pitch for the 68th. He promised her what he had available, but this was still not enough. Fry then introduced her to Governor Richard Yates of Illinois, and another coup for Agnes was in the making. Yates was a tough old fellow, but he succumbed to Agnes's persuasiveness, and promised her a company from Illinois.

He told Agnes, however,

> that he would not have it commanded by any 'New York bumpkin,' and proposed that he should make me captain of that company. He kept his word, and I received from him a captain's commission and captain's pay, which, he said, would assist me in defraying the expenses I incurred in assisting the sick and wounded soldiers, in whose treatment I was much interested.

Many other sources refer to the appointment of Agnes as a captain, so there must be some truth in the story, though one version has Yates giving her a captain's commission in honour of her hospital work. With this, the 68th now had a complement of nearly a thousand men, and on 8 June 1864 Felix with his new recruits joined the regiment in Bridgeport, Alabama.

⁂

Meanwhile, in September 1863, the 68th under Steinhausen, with the rest of the XI Corps (and the XII) under General Hooker, had been rushed west by rail from Virginia to confront a serious Confederate threat to Chattanooga, Tennessee.

Chattanooga, on the south bank of the Tennessee River, almost on the border with Georgia, was a vital railway junction and river port. The city is hemmed in by long steep mountain ridges that force the river into several sharp bends before it straightens out above Bridgeport, Alabama, and resumes its southwesterly course. When the Union army advanced on the city, the Confederates withdrew, lest they be trapped. After ferocious fighting, the Union forces were able to occupy and hold Chattanooga, but they in turn found themselves under siege by a formidable Confederate force south of the city.

Lincoln rushed reinforcements, General Hooker from Virginia with his two army corps and General William T. Sherman from the Mississippi valley. Overall command of the western armies was given to General Ulysses S. Grant. When Sherman's troops arrived, Grant attacked on 23 November. The Confederates were routed and the door to Georgia lay wide open. In early May 1864, Sherman and a hundred thousand men marched through that door toward Atlanta and, ultimately, the sea in a campaign that split the Confederacy in two.

The reinforcements from Virginia and Mississippi were rushed to Chattanooga by rail. The Union's overall superiority in railways was a decisive factor in its final victory. In the early years, America's far-flung river system provided the most effective mode of transport. Later came canals and, beginning in the 1840s, the railways. The floods of immigrants and settlers moving west and the necessity to open lines of ready transport between the Mid-West and the coast drove the rapid expansion of the railway network. The long lines of settler-laden wagons jolting west over dreadful roads were replaced by rail, and rail also carried troops to establish forts and guard the settlers in their new homes. Railways and bridges were thus vital for rapid troop movements, and their protection was a matter of great concern to the Union.

But it was obvious from Agnes's own movements that a determined lady could get a seat on a train if she persisted. And persist she did.

The 68th had fought hard in the defence of Chattanooga. It was now sent by rail to Bridgeport, Alabama, to guard the Nashville–Chattanooga Railroad against guerrilla attacks. All supplies for Chattanooga came by rail from Nashville via Bridgeport. The materiel needed by Sherman for his Georgia campaign was stockpiled in the depots and factories that sprang up along the river at Bridgeport. Such is the lie of the land that the railway from Nashville south cannot go directly to Chattanooga but must swing yet further south into Alabama and come up via Bridgeport. By rail, it was 26 miles from Bridgeport to Chattanooga. If the rail link was destroyed, it was a long haul over mountainous terrain on tracks that turned to mud in the rain. The railway bridge over the Tennessee River at Bridgeport was completed in 1854, but had been wrecked by rebels before the Union forces occupied the place in July 1863 and built a temporary pontoon bridge. The bridge and roadbed was wrecked again in a raid in April 1864, but was rebuilt by February of the next year.

The regimental headquarters of the 68th were established on a long narrow island in the Tennessee River, the southern end of which lies opposite Bridgeport. The railway bridge crossed (and still does) at this point. Bridgeport itself sits on a high bluff on the west bank of the river. Shipyards that turned out river steamers and the warehouses and factories stretched south and north of the town on flat land. High bluffs rise also on the east bank. The regimental camp was laid out in the middle of the island, just north of the railway bridge and line. Two blockhouses guarded the approaches to the camp, one on the island, the other facing it on the east bank.

While Lt Colonel von Steinhausen settled in on the island, Captain Baron von Fritsch opted to take command of the block-house on the south bank, which he occupied with 120 men of the 68th. He brought in furniture from Nashville, managed to secure some livestock, was able to buy some fresh provisions from the locals, and secured the services of a good cook, Mr Sutter, once in the service of the Duke of Nassau.

❦

Felix and his new recruits joined the rest of the 68th in June 1864. His superior officer was Colonel Wladimir Krzyzanowksi, commanding the 3rd Brigade of the Defense of the Nashville & Chattanooga Railroad. Krzyzanowski was a refugee from the Polish uprising in 1846. In New York in 1861 he organised the 58th New York Infantry Volunteers composed of Poles and Germans, and rose rapidly to the command of a brigade. He had been breveted[16] a brigadier general in November 1862, but the commission expired in March 1863 without the Senate having confirmed it. Carl Schurz, now a divisional commander, claimed it was because no one in the Senate could pronounce his name.

Agnes reached Nashville in July, accompanied by her maid and Jimmy, the terrier, but she missed Felix who had already gone on to Bridgeport. She tried every trick in her book, but for once was unable to follow him. The country was infested with guerrilla bands and was considered unsafe for travel. Not liking the accommodations at the St Cloud Hotel, she found lodging with a family in a nearby village, where Schurz had his headquarters.

Felix rode up for an eight-day visit, but would not hear of her going back to Bridgeport with him. She reluctantly agreed to return to Washington until such time as he sent for her. The summer passed before he deemed conditions safe enough.

In the meantime, in May General Sherman had launched from Chattanooga the campaign that ended with the capture of Atlanta in September. His next move was to march to the sea at Savannah. To disrupt his plans, the Confederacy sent General John B. Hood westward around the Union flank and back toward Nashville. Sherman in turn ordered General George H. Thomas to return to Tennessee to keep an eye on Hood and assorted raiders. General James B. Steedman was sent with him to take command of a provisional corps of some 5000 men in Chattanooga. The corps was a very mixed bag of soldiers from different units, stragglers, invalids and eight regiments of black troops. It also contained a brigade commanded by one Benjamin Harrison, who would one day become the twenty-third president of the US.

On 1 October 1864, Agnes and Mrs Corvin left Washington in a stateroom on a sleeping car. How she managed this she does not say. By train and ferry they proceeded to Pittsburgh, Cincinnati, Louisville and finally Nashville in a relentless rain. The St Cloud Hotel was full of officers, but Agnes knew the owner and managed in her usual way to get a room. Trains ran only sporadically south to Bridgeport, and guerrillas roamed the country practising, according to Agnes, the most awful cruelties on prisoners.

Nothing daunted, she talked their way onto a train due to leave for Bridgeport. With the assistance of a captain she knew, she and Mrs Corvin were soon comfortably ensconced and on their way. Unfortunately, an officious guard suddenly put them off, saying women had no place on a troop train, and they faced a disagreeable few minutes before some officers she knew smuggled them into a car. They were very uncomfortable, and the weather continued awful, but at least they were moving in the right direction.

The train ran through dense woods and hills where guerrillas might lurk, and stopped frequently, which added to the general uneasiness. Along the tracks lay wrecked and burned cars and locomotives.

Agnes had drifted off to sleep when Mrs Corvin suddenly aroused her with the news that Jimmy had jumped off the train. She could see the unfortunate dog trying to catch up, so she pulled the emergency cord.

> The train stopped, and the captain who was in command ran anxiously to ask what accident had happened. On hearing it he was inclined to be angry, but seeing my distress, and probably being a lover of dogs himself, he relaxed; the train stopped until my pet arriving panting from such an unusual exertion, and amid the good-natured laughter of the soldiers the dear deserter was returned to me.

One can only imagine what the captain had to say when he got back to his locomotive.

When they arrived at Bridgeport station, about a mile and a half from Felix's camp, soldiers found an ambulance and some breakfast, and in no time she was once again at her husband's side.

Captain Fritsch now takes up the story. Agnes mentions not a word about Fritsch, who clearly disliked the Salms, but he did make an effort to get into her good graces – to protect himself if for no other reason. Agnes was rumoured to have blocked the advancement of officers whom she saw as standing in her husband's way.

> The most unpleasant day was when Prince Salm-Salm arrived on the island, followed by his wife, two other ladies, and some seven men to whom he had promised commissions in the

Regiment. The officers and men received him with sour faces, but as I had known him in Germany, when he was an officer in the Prussian Hussars, and he and I had moved during one winter in the same society at Frankfort-on-the-Main, where he frequently led the cotillion, I was obliged to greet him in a friendly manner, and invited him, his ladies and suite, to dine at my cottage, placing my accommodations at his disposal until the Quartermaster was able to fix a place for him.

This gave me a chance to become acquainted with his most beautiful, charming and accomplished wife, of whose deeds of valor in former campaigns I had already heard, and who had many times attended the wounded on battlefields.

Fritsch gives a version of Agnes's past that demonstrates how successful she was in confusing the issue and letting rumour grow thick.

From what I could hear, this lady was the daughter of a former English Colonel, who, being a passionate hunter, had left the service and joined the Hudson Bay Fur Company. For years he lived in the far West of Canada as a nimrod [hunter], and there married a very pretty Indian squaw, daughter of a chief and known as 'The Princess'. When quite young his daughter was stolen by some Indian enemy and sold to a circus manager, who had noticed her riding a wild bronco on the plains. He took her away with him to Cuba and South America, and after a time she became the most daring rider of bareback horses, and attracted much attention on account of her brilliant eyes and lovely form. Still, this is only one version of her first life, and it may not be true at all.

The bare facts are all there, but they have been artfully rearranged.

Besides her great beauty, the Princess was known for her remarkably free and easy manners, her determined ways and daring horsemanship, and of course other ladies considered her a mere adventuress; but in reality she was only a very shrewd woman, whose motto was the same as that of the Jesuits: 'The end justifies the means'.

She was never vulgar, but blushed easily, and often showed that at heart she was a most respectable little woman. Naturally, she made use of her charms, and bestowed her favors on those who could promote her husband's interests. Proud and politely cold with ordinary men, she was seductive only with influential people and very personal friends.

He was much harsher on Felix, whom he had known for years, particularly on his extravagance and constant borrowing of money.

> In spite of my kind reception and hospitality, and knowing that by his damnable appointment as Colonel in my Regiment, he had killed my well-deserved chances for promotion, he borrowed a hundred dollars from me 'until the next pay day'. The very next morning he told me that he must create vacancies in the Regiment for seven of his friends, as he was under great obligations to them, and could only reward them by commissions in the 68th.

With extraordinary arrogance, he insisted to Fritsch that the present officers of the 68th must resign, from Steinhausen on down. There were heated quarrels, and finally three lieutenants resigned in disgust. That made three places for his friends, but Steinhausen, the major and the captains refused to give way. They had fought hard to earn their promotions, and were not about to give way. Meanwhile, Felix had to feed his friends and keep them in cigars and wine. He tried everything to get Fritsch to go back east and seek a colonel's appointment, more suitable to one of his background than a mere captaincy, but Fritsch was not to be persuaded. He was quite happy, he said, guarding his bridges.

Fritsch was only too aware, however, that he might be in danger, and resolved to butter up Agnes. He had escorted her, driven her in his buggy, presented her with the freshest vegetables – nothing worked. So he decided to throw a party in her honour. He prepared meticulously. Everyone was invited: General Thomas and staff, General Steedman and staff, Colonel Prince Salm and staff. The fourteenth of November 1864 was the day. The afternoon entertainment opened with cocktails, interrupted by a sham attack on Blockhouse L, Fritsch's headquarters. The soldiers jumped to their guns and beat off the mock attackers. The demonstration was a great success, if a bit smoky.

> In two tents – one for the ladies and one for the officers – toilet accommodations had been provided, and brand new tin basins and gorgeous looking glasses gave everyone an opportunity to wash and fix up. Then we entered an immense hospital tent, loaned to me by the Quartermaster at Nashville.

> All my guests were seated at a large table, covered with snow white linen, porcelain plates, fine glassware, napkins, etc., loaned to me for the occasion by a hotel man in Nashville.
>
> A lovely doll formed the centre piece, representing and actually resembling the Princess, with her big eyes, such as Byron gave to his Haidee, and Poe to his lost Leonora, with cheeks that reflected the glow of health, and a costume that showed all the refinement of fashionable society. She was surrounded by beautiful flowers, and excited much admiration.

The chef outdid himself. There were oysters, consommé, fish patties, roasted wild turkeys, salads, preserves, and a rich desert, French coffee and fine cigars. Sherry, Pontet Canet, Rhine wine and champagne accompanied the repast that was served by 20 soldiers in white jackets. Fritsch proposed a flattering toast to Agnes, in which the company joined amidst great applause.

Military drills took up the late afternoon, and when dusk fell, Chinese lanterns illuminated the grounds and a cold supper was served. From generals on down, everyone was delighted.

> The dear Princess was the last to leave. She went in the cele-brated buggy, transformed for this day into a bower of roses. She thanked me several times, and took a very affectionate leave of me at the Pontoon Bridge, the outskirt of my post. 'I will stick to you through thick and thin,' she said. 'Just come to me when you get into trouble.' I sighed, as if desperately in love, and kissed her delicate hand.

All this was laid on by a captain in a fairly remote post in northern Alabama in the middle of a civil war with the roads supposedly teeming with guerrillas. It was to no avail; Agnes mentions not one word of any of this.

Fritsch knew too much about Felix and his past. He had not knuckled under when Felix wanted to replace the old and tested officers of the 68th with his own chums. He had refused to go back east as Felix had suggested. He was, in short, part of the opposition to Felix that had surfaced back in New York in 1863, and Agnes, fiercely loyal to her husband, did not like him. She also disliked Steinhausen for much the same reason. They and their kind had no place in her memoirs.

The episode does Felix no credit. The 'great obligations' to his friends to which Fritsch referred were presumably debts, indicating that Felix had not mended his spendthrift ways. It also shows his extraordinary insensitivity to interests other than his own. His efforts to get rid of a seasoned crew of officers must have seriously hampered his ability to be an able regimental commander, but this seems not to have bothered him. Agnes appears to have supported him in these manoeuvres. She was always loyal to her Felix, though she must have been aware of the costs of his highhandedness.

On the island, the Salms had put together their own dwelling. It was some 30 feet long, erected on pilings to avoid occasional flooding, and had a veranda and three main rooms, a living-room plus two bedrooms, one for the Salms and one for Mrs Corvin. The living-room had a glass door and two windows, and a fireplace 'of rather primitive construction, for when it rained hard the fire was frequently extinguished'. The island was flat and subject to flooding, but there were lovely trees, lots of birds, many with brilliant plumage, and two or three farms. In rainy weather, it was not particularly pleasant, but when the sun shone it was a delightful place. A sawmill in Bridgeport provided lumber, and the camp had wooden structures as well as tents.

Agnes speaks with sympathy of the plight of the farmers on the island whose destitute families came in search of food, especially salt used to cure pork. They rode on miserable animals not requisitioned by war, and were in rags. Humiliated at having to beg, 'they all behaved, however, with a certain dignity which did not fail to produce a favourable effect on our soldiers, who generally treated them with kindness'. Agnes's heart usually went out to the poor and unfortunate. With all else, she was a kindly and caring woman whose instincts were to get in there and help when she saw misery and injustice.

Fritsch alludes to the work Agnes did with the wounded on battlefields. In fact, her strong suit was in organising hospital care and in bringing together the necessary supplies and provisions rather than actual battlefield nursing. She proved to be a brilliant organiser. Her hospital work became very important to her, and she was very good at it.

Measures for the care of the sick and wounded were rudimentary at the outbreak of the war. The Medical Bureau of the War Department was unprepared for casualties on any scale, and was, by all accounts, hopelessly inefficient. Hospitals existed in Washington, and civilians, particularly ladies, helped in a variety of ways. Ladies' relief societies sprang up all over the country, but their efforts and the goods and material they collected were not in any way coordinated. In the field it was worse. Ambulances were cumbersome four-wheeled wagons drawn by four horses, providing an excruciating ride for the sorely wounded. Railway cars were pressed into service, as were ships, to bring the wounded into Washington. A corps of nurses was developing, following the example set by Florence Nightingale in the Crimean War (1854–56), and in June 1861 Dorothy Dix of Massachusetts was appointed Superintendent of Women Nurses. She and her nurses faced a wall of male hostility, especially from the medical profession.

A group of clergymen and doctors in New York, shocked by the loss of life to disease during the Crimean War, determined to establish a scientific board that would have the power to enforce sanitary regulations in the camps. They persisted in the teeth of opposition from the Medical Bureau, and the United States Sanitary Commission (USSC) gradually took shape. While the organisers set to work in the summer of 1861 raising funds, the executive duties fell to the General Secretary of the USSC, one Frederick Law Olmsted, who took leave from his project laying out Central Park in New York City to work tirelessly at this new mission.

The USSC was a huge success. Supplies poured into enormous storehouses and were distributed where they were needed. Some 500 trained agents moved wagon-loads of supplies to hospitals and camps. Field ambulances, nurses, convalescent camps, care for discharged soldiers – nothing escaped them. Starting with Chicago in October 1863, the USSC hit on the idea of holding 'sanitary fairs' in major cities to raise money and encourage donations in kind. The whole effort also, not incidentally, brought women out of their homes and into action, surprising their male colleagues with their ability to serve on committees, raise money and play generally useful roles. Credit should also be given to the Christian Commission organised late in 1861 by the YMCA that worked closely with the USSC.

Agnes was in the thick of the action. One of the first things she did was to visit the camp hospital on the island, which she found in miserable condition. She thought the doctor was slip-shod and more concerned with his own perquisites and comfort than that of his patients. The administrators and nurses were no better; she discovered that they frequently appropriated things meant for the sick. Indignant at this state of affairs, she set to work at once. From the agents of the Christian Commission in Bridgeport, she procured warm clothes, shoes, blankets and decent rations for the patients, the worst off of whom she had transferred to the larger hospital in Bridgeport. The soldiers had run very short of provisions, and the contributions of the Christian Commission were very useful, though they had to be satisfied with salt pork and hard tack, for bread was also in short supply. Felix and the officers supplemented their meagre fare with partridges and wild pigeons shot on the island.

In her memoirs, Agnes sharply criticised the treatment of soldiers during the Franco–Prussian War and the callous way the dead were treated. She went on to say, 'It is true that in the American war it occurred not rarely that the wounded had to be left behind, that they perished miserably, that the dead could not be buried at all or only in haste, so that bodies were dug out by the pigs, as I have seen happen here and there; but such cases are to be avoided, and are exceptions; wherever there was a possibility, the dead were treated with respect and love'. The dead were collected and identified and then carefully buried, not thrown into common pits. Many were sent home in metal coffins. The government established public war cemeteries and kept them maintained.

And then there was the social whirl. Trips across the river to Bridgeport were dangerous, and the roads were often quagmires, but they had frequent visitors all the same, gave dinner parties and generally had company in the evening. They played whist 'and Groeben brewed a very acceptable eggnog or punch, for the wine furnished by our sutler, though charged three dollars a bottle and provided with flourishing labels, was a miserable compound'. Major General James Steedman, commander in Chattanooga, dined with them on 23 October and invited them to visit him in Chattanooga. Four days later, the Salms, Mrs Corvin and Groeben set out seated in a transport wagon. The ride was uncomfortable, but the scenery made up for it, in part.

> The road to Chattanooga is very romantic, leading through a fine but rather wild-looking mountainous country, and over bridges which make me still shudder in thinking of them. The rebels had destroyed the good and solid ones, and they had provisionally been replaced by others, built in the greatest haste by the soldiers. There was especially one, known as the Match-bridge, which surpassed anything I ever saw or heard of. It crossed a deep and wide gorge, and was built of wood – trellis work – several hundred feet high, in three stories. When the train passed over it the whole flimsy fabric swayed in the most alarming manner.

It took eight hours to reach Chattanooga, where General Steedman received them and escorted them to their hotel. The party set off for Lookout Mountain at nine in the morning of the twenty-sixth, Mrs Corvin and Groeben in a wagon, the rest on horseback. At the last minute, Steedman sent word he could not come, General Sherman having ordered him to ready troops to go to Decatur, Alabama, but he sent his adjutant as a guide.

Agnes described Lookout Mountain as 'an enormous rock, rising like a citadel from the valley of the Lookout Creek'. It had been the scene of the famous 'battle above the clouds' that broke the siege of Chattanooga. It is, in fact, an enormous north–south ridge, looming some 1500 feet over the city, with an almost sheer face to the west, up which the battle was fought. The picnickers selected their spot and settled down on the moss 'to enjoy the exquisite breakfast which General Steedman had sent up, together with a good supply of champagne, which

made us all very merry'. They were back in Chattanooga by
7.00 p.m.

The next day Agnes and Mrs Corvin went around to the
Sanitary Commission, which gave them a quantity of useful provisions. The needs of the Chattanooga hospitals were great, but
'the provisions of the Commission seemed inexhaustible and they
never grew tired of giving with full hands'. They paid Steedman
a farewell visit and lunched with him before returning to the hotel
to pack up. Several generals were presented to them, but 'they
were all rather busy, for we saw five thousand men passing our
window on the way to Decatur'. They left Chattanooga at four
and were back in Bridgeport without incident.

⚜

The sudden troop movements were necessitated by the appear-
ance at the gates of Tennessee of the Confederate General John
B. Hood. As previously noted, with Atlanta in Union hands
(September 1864) and Sherman readying for his march across
Georgia to Savannah on the sea, the Confederate command
had dispatched Hood to skirt around the western flank of the
Union forces. Sherman, anticipating some such move, had
sent Thomas and Steedman back to Tennessee at the end of
September, and Hood had to withdraw south and west. One of
Hood's purposes was to impede Union troop movements by
disrupting and destroying as many railways and bridges as
possible, but his main goal was Nashville. He moved west along
the Tennessee River looking for a crossing, but the bridges were
firmly in Union hands.

Steedman was a controversial figure. Regular army officers
regarded him as the worst kind of political officer, and his fondness for gambling, alcohol and women was widely known and
deplored. He was the owner of the *Toledo Times* (Ohio), had
served in the Ohio legislature and had failed in a bid for
Congress. On the other hand, he had volunteered in the
Mexican War and in 1849 had joined the gold rush to California.
In 1861 he became colonel of the 14th Ohio Volunteers, being
promoted to brigadier general in July 1862 and major general

49

in April 1864. He was a large, imposing man of tremendous bravery and physical courage, but allegedly indifferent to the welfare of his troops, whom he drove hard. His prompt action at a critical moment during the battle for Chattanooga helped save the day for the Union. Steedman personally rallied his inexperienced troops by seizing a regimental standard and rushing to the attack.

Typical of those who disliked him was Major General David S. Stanley, a West Pointer. In October 1864, Stanley wrote,

> Chattanooga was commanded by General James Steedman, the most thorough specimen of a political general I met during the war. He always managed to hold command where there were emoluments. At this time he was living in very high style, holding a gay court. The Princess Salm-Salm was his guest, and occasionally the Prince, who was the colonel of a New York regiment stationed twenty miles from headquarters, dropped in. The Princess was a very beautiful woman, afterwards mixed up with the tragedy of Maximilian. Steedman was dead in love with the woman, and such an idiot that I could not get any work out of him. In fact he was so taken up with making love to the Princess and drinking champagne that it was difficult to see this great potentate of Chattanooga.[17]

On 26 October 1864, Felix in Bridgeport sent a curious telegram to General Thomas: 'General: I hereby have the honor most respectfully to apply to be transferred from the command of Colonel W. Krzyzanowski and to be assigned to an American brigade in the Department of the Cumberland'. The 68th had been in Krzyzanowski's 3rd Brigade since July. The choice of words – 'an American brigade' – is odd. Does this reflect the serious internal divisions in the 68th between Felix and most of the other officers described by Captain Fritsch? Did he, or Agnes, resent Krzyzanowski's success? Or did Felix simply want to see action? Whatever the reason, Steedman endorsed the request on 31 October, noting, 'I have no doubt but that this change would advance the interest of the service'.

In all fairness, Felix must have felt keenly that most of his fellow officers had seen serious action while he had not. Disliking him as they did, they probably missed no opportunity to remind him.

On 28 October, he was ordered to join General Thomas without delay on an expedition to destroy the pontoon bridge over the Tennessee River west of Decatur. They were too late. Hood got his men across, but then had to wait until supplies were brought up and to give his men a rest. He resumed his advance toward Nashville on 20 November.

Steedman and his corps were ordered to join Thomas in Nashville and to leave only a skeleton force to protect the posts between Stevenson and Chattanooga. Felix was perishing to take part in the impending battle, and on his request Steedman attached him to his staff.

Steedman telegraphed that he would arrive in the afternoon with his troops. Felix and the 68th prepared to join him. The Salms waited in the port commander's quarters 'where we whiled away the time with eating and drinking Catawba champagne, for the trains kept us waiting until eleven o'clock p.m.' The general had eleven trains, crammed with troops. Agnes and the Corvins were expecting, rather optimistically, that the road to Nashville would soon be open, and they made plans to leave for Washington a few days later. 'We therefore were by no means agreeably surprised,' she wrote, 'on hearing from the general that the train which he brought with him was the last running, and that we would have to wait in Bridgeport until General Hood was defeated.' Still, the apparent ease with which civilians could get about on trains in the midst of all this is remarkable.

The cold was bitter and the rain freezing at the beginning of December. A fierce ice storm delayed Hood's progress as he doggedly fought his way north into Tennessee. A thaw and warm rain now turned the countryside into a sea of mud. The forces of Thomas and Steedman were drawn up before Nashville, awaiting Hood's approach. Felix was on Steedman's staff, and the impending battle was to be his first really serious engagement.

The battle of Nashville was fought over two days, 15 and 16 December 1864, and ended in a Confederate rout. Hood's army was virtually destroyed and the remnants evacuated Tennessee. Steedman's division joined in the pursuit of the broken Confederate army, but sheer exhaustion brought them to a halt. Four days after Nashville, far away on the coast, the Confederates abandoned Savannah to Sherman's advancing army.

Sheer exhaustion and the weather: rain, sleet, snow, freezing winds and mud, mud, mud continued to plague the whole region, making troop movements a nightmare.

Stuck in Bridgeport, Agnes did her best to pass the time as agreeably as possible. Various general officers came to call, and Corvin and Groeben astonished them 'by the wonderful punch which they brewed from commissariat whisky, with the help of lemon-peel, preserved pineapples, Vanilla essence, and sugar'. General Gordon Granger invited them to visit him in Stevenson, another important railhead south of Bridgeport, expeditions that 'were not without danger, and perhaps for that reason more tempting'. Granger was a dashing cavalry officer who, with Steedman, had played a decisive role in the defence of Chattanooga.

As was her usual style, whenever she and her companions needed transportation for some outing Agnes sent a wire to her friend General Thomas Meagher in Chattanooga to let them have the loan of a locomotive. He always came through, despite the grumblings of his transportation department. Meagher generally sent a locomotive with a car attached, sometimes one transport wagon. Stevenson was only ten miles away, but the road passed through woods where there was danger of guerrillas. Agnes took the precaution of taking along some regimental soldiers, well armed, who sat on top of the wagon to keep watch. Such are the perquisites of the commander's wife. Despite the discomforts and perils, the trips were worth the effort, since Granger was considered a *bon vivant* and was famous for his dinners, always accompanied by band music.

Finally came news of the great victory at Nashville, and all rejoiced, though there was a brief scare that elements of Hood's army might fall on them. Two gunboats were brought up to protect the island. When Agnes learned that Steedman and 15 trains of troops would arrive at Stevenson on 23 December, she rushed to meet them.

> Steedman and Salm looked more like robbers than officers, for they had gone through hard times and had no leisure to think of their toilet. Their beards were more than a week old, and their uniforms covered with mud and torn to rags…Salm was beaming with happiness, not alone on account of our

meeting, but because he at last has had fighting to his heart's content, and an opportunity to distinguish himself. During the battle Steedman had given him a command, and could not find words enough to praise his bravery and good behavior.

Steedman now promised to give Felix command of a brigade, and recommend to Thomas that he be promoted.

They were back home in Bridgeport for Christmas, and the weather improved for a moment. They decked their halls with holly from the woods and had a jolly Christmas Eve. Corvin brewed gallons of whisky punch, there was a piano, and they sang and danced into the night. On Christmas Day the Salms entertained in a like vein at their house.

Meanwhile, Agnes had not lost sight of her priorities. While Felix was with Steedman before Nashville, she paid a visit to Fritsch. She told him that Felix had been attached to Steedman's staff and that Steedman intended to form a brigade for him and recommend to Thomas that he be appointed a brevet brigadier. Furthermore, she said, when Felix was a full brigadier, 'I promise you that I will go at once to Albany and ask the Governor to make you Colonel of the 68th Regiment, as I hate that old Lieutenant Colonel [Steinhausen] ... I will explain all this to the Governor, and I invariably succeed when I put my war paint on.'

General Steedman now did give Felix command of a reserve brigade, while still commanding the 68th, and on 8 January 1865 Felix assumed command of the Bridgeport post.

The battle at Nashville had been decisive, but it was not the end of the story in the rugged hills and mountains of Tennessee and Alabama. After the battle, the Confederates rather optimistically assigned General Hylan B. Lyon, a Kentuckian born and bred, to the command of enemy-occupied western Kentucky. Raising recruits, harassing Union forces and wrecking the railways were his main objectives. Felix and a number of others spent considerable time and energy searching for Lyon, who was darting about with a variously estimated number of men in the triangle formed by the great bend in the Tennessee River south of the Alabama–Tennessee border. Rumoured sightings were followed by quick marches, but the rebel general always seemed to fade away as the Union forces approached. The weather had turned ugly again, and the reports on these operations make clear the vital importance of the railways for moving troops in areas where the roads were bad at the best of times and impossible in the kind of weather they were experiencing.

There was a flurry of excitement on 8 January 1865 when it was learned that Lyon was in the vicinity with 500 men and attempting to get across the Tennessee River. Thomas's orders were to destroy Lyon's forces and prevent his escape. The various brigades, including Felix's, fanned out over the countryside in pursuit. The weather was terrible: rain pouring down, streams flooded, mud deep. The chase went on for three days, as did the bad weather, but in the end Lyon managed to get away.

The general commanding the operation paid tribute in his report to Steedman's headquarters to the behaviour of officers and men alike under the terrible mid-winter conditions. He then singled out brigade commanders for praise, including Colonel Felix Prince Salm of the 68th New York, Commanding Reserve Brigade, who was commended 'for the zeal, energy, and good sense which he brings to the service of the Government'.[18]

Felix himself wrote a report from Bridgeport on 17 January 1865 to the Adjutant General at headquarters in Chattanooga describing his pursuit of a force of rebel cavalry west of Bridgeport through very rough country in the rain and mud. There were skirmishes with rebel bands, but the main body of the force got away.

Agnes, in the meantime, had left Bridgeport with the Corvins for Nashville, where they stayed again at the St Cloud. She doubtless relished some relief from the island, but learning that Felix was due back with his brigade, she managed to find a hospital train going her way and was back at the camp when Felix arrived on 13 January. The Corvins went on to Washington. Agnes threw herself into hospital work again. She inspected the local facilities and found them suffering from neglect, so she had to go to Chattanooga to round up supplies. General Steedman proved helpful with loading the material she had collected into a hospital train for the return trip. She waxed eloquent about the spacious and airy American hospital trains, well provided with the hospital equipment and comforts needed by the wounded and the surgeons who treated them.

By this time, the Salms were no longer living on the island, but had moved to the post commander's quarters on the highest point in Bridgeport, with beautiful views up and down the Tennessee River.

All was not calm, however. Guerrillas and fragments of the Confederate army still riddled the area, especially south of the Tennessee River. Felix had to chase them out and defend against raids.

On 27 January he surprised a rebel camp with a detachment of the 68th, and there was a sharp skirmish. The rugged wooded terrain hampered his movements, and in the end the greater part of the rebels escaped. He lost one lieutenant; the enemy lost one killed, eight wounded and four captured. He took a quantity of arms and equipment. The 68th was attacked the next day, but repulsed the band with no losses.

On 7 February he left on a two-day expedition across the river into the Raccoon Mountains west of Bridgeport. Three days later he came upon a good-sized rebel band. In the skirmish Felix and his men killed three of the enemy, wounded five and captured a captain from Georgia and 15 men. The clash also netted a considerable number of arms and 23 horses. Steedman reported the action to Thomas's army headquarters, along with another recommendation for promotion. In virtually every report he sent to Thomas on his subordinate, Steedman praised Felix's sterling qualities and recommended a promotion. One can detect Agnes's influence at work, but Felix was trying his best.

Agnes was cheered in the middle of February when her sister Delia and husband Captain Johnson arrived. Johnson had been attached to Felix's brigade.

The campaign to secure Felix a promotion to brigadier general had been underway for some time, but Agnes was not at all satisfied with its progress. She had also interested herself in the careers of several other officers. There was a hitch somewhere, and she suspected hostile influences at work in Washington.

There was no point in twiddling her thumbs in Bridgeport. Washington was the place to be.

Agnes recognised that her husband's promotion to brigadier general depended in the first instance on Secretary of War Stanton, who had to propose him to the Senate for confirmation. Though Stanton was known to be less than enthusiastic about foreign officers in the army, she also knew he could not disregard the recommendations of influential governors or senators. Stanton required their support for other purposes, and she looked forward to somehow arranging an exchange of favours that would benefit Felix. By this time she had any number of highly placed friends, and she was confident that she could persuade them to back Felix. It was vital, however, to secure recommendations from generals in the field.

Steedman approved of her plans and, accompanied by Groeben, she set off for Washington on 24 February ready to fight for the interests of Felix and the brigade.

She arrived in Washington on 6 March. The Senate was due to adjourn at the end of the week. Time was short. The next day, therefore, she called on Senators Ira Harris of New York, Henry Wilson of New Hampshire and James Nesmick of Oregon, plus Generals Hooker and Fry in the War Department. It helped that Wilson was the chairman of the Senate Committee on Military Affairs and Nesmick a member. Hooker she had known for a long time and Fry had helped the Salms with his appointment to the 68th.

Hooker had in fact already joined those praising Felix. He had written to Thomas on 15 February:

> Colonel Salm commanded the 8th New York Regiment, in the XI Corps, at the time I was in command of the Army of the Potomac, with great credit. He is a good disciplinarian, and while with his Regiment was thoroughly acquainted with administration and discipline. He was zealous in the performance of his duties, and always efficient. The reports of his commanders in the Army of the Cumberland sustain the good character he had acquired in the Army of the Potomac.

This was praise from a very significant quarter. Steedman may have been derided as a political hack and reprobate, but Hooker was a towering figure, above reproach.

From Fry, who kept her advised of how the business of Felix was proceeding within the War Department, she learned that Stanton would not forward Felix's nomination to the Senate without a firm recommendation from General Thomas.

Agnes organised her forces, and in late March the telegrams flew. A key figure in her network was her old friend Richard Yates, formerly governor of Illinois and now senator from that state. Steedman telegraphed his support of Felix to Yates, who forwarded it to Stanton. Yates requested Thomas to send his recommendations to Stanton. Finally, on 23 March Agnes herself weighed in with a personal note to Stanton: 'I feel very anxious to know your decision in the case of my husband, Colonel Salm. I desire to leave for Nashville as soon as I get his commission. May I call for it this morning?'[19] She went to the War Department in person, but Stanton was too busy to see her, so she sent in her note. Ever determined, she wrote in her diary on 27 March, 'I feel very unhappy, but I will succeed, even if it kills me'.

She was beside herself with worry, but she opened a new front. Having done all she could with the military, she decided to enlist the governors of New York and New Hampshire (the 68th included some New Hampshire troops). The more pressure she could bring on Stanton, the better. She fired off a wire to Governor Joseph Gilmore of New Hampshire and set off directly for Albany with Groeben in tow. When she reached New York Governor Reuben Fenton's office, she found him sympathetic, and he promised to do his best. There was also the matter of the other 68th regimental promotions Agnes had promised to shepherd, and Fenton took care of those as well. She sent Groeben back to Bridgeport with these commissions, while she returned to Washington. A dispatch from Gilmore also promised support.

Back in the nation's capital, she lodged with the Corvins in Georgetown and awaited events.

Stanton was trying to run a war, and was doubtless infuriated by this kind of pressuring, but in the end Agnes and her legions wore him down. She called on Senator Yates on 10 April and heard good news: General Thomas had informed him that he had recommended Felix for a promotion. Yates promised her he would see Stanton on the twelfth. 'I called on the Senator on Thursday, the 13th of April, and was never happier in my life, for Yates delivered into my hands the commission of general for Felix, signed by Stanton. How proud I felt when I sent a dispatch to Bridgeport addressed to General Felix Salm!' The brevet of 13 April named Felix Prince Salm a brigadier general commanding the 2nd Brigade of the 2nd Separate Division, Department of the Etowah (Steedman), Army of the Cumberland (Thomas).

Agnes then let herself go in a rather revealing and patronising paragraph.

> Yes, I felt extremely happy and proud. He had given me his name and made me a princess, but notwithstanding his name and rank he would have failed after his first start, and remained a colonel without a regiment, involved as he was in the fate of poor Blenker. All his merit would have availed him little against the rancour of Stanton. I procured for him the command of the 8th, and raised for him the 68th Regiment; now he had become a general through my exertions.

One occasionally has the sense that Agnes saw Felix as a work in progress and a vehicle through which she could obtain the kind of life she sought. She was immensely ambitious, almost driven, and was determined to propel Felix to the top. Some have seen an almost maternal streak in her love for him, but the reality was that she was a 'take charge' type and Felix needed tending. From the very beginning she had assumed responsibility for his career. He fought; she ran the show. She had indeed done all the high-level work to get him his two regiments and her relentless campaign to have him promoted to brigadier general was planned and executed with remarkable skill and persistence. She had learned the ropes and just how to pull them. Besides, there can be no doubt that Agnes thoroughly enjoyed playing the game. It was what she was best at.

But it was all a bit too late. Richmond, capital of the Confederacy, fell to General Grant on 3 April. General Robert E. Lee surrendered to Grant on 9 April. And President Abraham Lincoln was assassinated on 14 April.

5

Brigadier General Felix Prince Salm

Felix finally had the rank for which Agnes had worked so hard and for which, it is fair to say, he had done his bit. General Order no 65 of the Adjutant General's Office, War Department, dated 22 June 1867, noted that Felix was promoted for 'meritorious service at the battle of Nashville, Tenn., effective 13 April 1865'. He had received numerous commendations along the way, and no one could ever criticise him for lack of courage. He just was not given very much of a glamourous nature to do.

Steinhausen, the Lt Colonel whom Agnes did not like, assumed command of the 68th. Fritsch remained a captain. They were not on Agnes's list for promotion.

At the beginning of May, Felix and his brigade moved to Dalton, Georgia, northwest of Atlanta. Steedman had been appointed military governor of Georgia, and he and his command set to the task of mopping up and restoring civil authority.

Poor Felix found himself involved now in activities for which he had no training and most probably no inclination whatsoever. On 15 May he sent a somewhat plaintive report to headquarters on his efforts to re-establish civil authority among local civilians. He had tried to organise a meeting to nominate delegates for local government at Spring Place, a town east of Dalton, but the citizens ripped the notices down and declared they would have nothing to do with any laws of the federal government.

Meanwhile Agnes had been busy as usual. She was always looking ahead, and had set her sights on Andrew Johnson, now president. She had met Johnson at the St Cloud Hotel in Nashville while he was military governor of Tennessee. Always on the lookout for a new figure in power who might have his uses some day, she decided to renew their acquaintance and went to call on him. She found him 'much occupied', however, but he sent word that he would receive her on 24 April. This was ten days after Lincoln's assassination and one can well imagine that Johnson was 'much occupied'.

When Agnes showed up at the appointed time, the room was too crowded for her to speak what was on her mind, but the President invited her to return after business hours the same day. This she did, but – maddeningly – she does not say what they discussed. Being in the good graces of the new president was to be more valuable to the Salms a couple of years later than they could have dreamed at the time.

She was in Louisville, Kentucky in mid-May, and then made arrangements to join Felix in Dalton. She described the trip from Chattanooga to Dalton as a horrible one, over ruined railways. This trip quickly became part of the Agnes lore, for she rode outside on the cow-catcher of the train with the well-travelled Jimmy on her lap.

Her sister Delia and her husband were now stationed in Cleveland, Tennessee, just east of Chattanooga. Delia was expecting another child, and Agnes suddenly revealed a rare flash of emotion. She wrote that she 'felt very envious, for I had no child which made me quite unhappy'. In an extraordinary move, Delia promised Agnes that she could have the child if it were a boy. When the wire came that the birth was imminent, Agnes set out in a horse-drawn ambulance. It was only 25 miles to Cleveland, but she and the driver had an awful time in violent thunderstorms. When she arrived, Delia greeted her with a baby boy 'who therefore was to be mine,' exulted Agnes. The child was named Felix Salm-Salm Johnson.

Agnes returned to Dalton and on 3 July Delia arrived with the baby. 'I was extremely happy to have at last a baby, and it became the centre around which everything turned – even my pet Jimmy was neglected.' A nurse was engaged to take care of the child.

One can only speculate why the Salms had had no children. They clearly loved each other and, insofar as possible during the war, had made a good life for themselves. They worried about each other when they were apart. Felix was an attentive husband who took great pains, for example, in setting up and furnishing their tent at Aquia Creek and again on the island off Bridgeport. He took care of niceties when he could – witness the mirror he managed to get for her at Aquia Creek. He was a prince and she was now a princess, and Felix knew something about living in style; perhaps too much, given his known extravagance. Agnes was perhaps a bit obsessive about Felix's promotion, but she was doing it for his sake as well as hers. They were in this together.

But he was also headstrong and opinionated, focused on being a good soldier and commander. Very possibly he did not want to be encumbered with a child. A child would also have tied Agnes down and inhibited her movements. At the outset, also, Agnes was a social butterfly and perhaps not ready to start a family. I suspect that in the turmoil of war they just put it off and then put it off some more. Delia's good fortune suddenly brought home to Agnes what she had missed.

But the moment passed and little Felix is never mentioned again. He must have been returned to his mother. The Salms were off again.

General Sherman was transferred to Augusta, Georgia, and on 7 July 1865 he named Felix commander of the Atlanta Military District. They moved the same day. Delia's husband Edmund Johnson was appointed Assistant Provost-Marshal, and they too transferred to Augusta.

Finding a place to live in the ruins of Atlanta was not easy for the Salms, but a few days later they had a nice house that Felix could also use as his headquarters. (The Lawshe house, as it is now known, still stands on Peachtree Street, between Cain and Harris.) The ruin of Atlanta was a deliberate act of General Sherman. He marched out of Chattanooga on 5 May 1864 and had to fight hard for every one of the 90 miles that separated him from Atlanta. The city was fiercely defended, and not till the end of July could Sherman clamp a vice around it. The Confederate commander, General John Hood, was forced to evacuate the city on 2 September.

Sherman ruthlessly cleared Atlanta of all civilians, the better to defend it. The situation was still dangerous, with strong Confederate armies in the field. When Sherman set off on his march across Georgia to the sea at Savannah, he ordered Atlanta fired – railway depots, warehouses, factories, stores – anything the Confederates might possibly use if they retook the city. On 16 November he set out for the coast, destroying everything in his path. Savannah fell on 20 December.

Agnes was horrified at the conditions they found in Atlanta, and had harsh words for Sherman's draconian orders expelling the civilian population and putting the town to the torch. She also condemned the barbarous behaviour of many of the Federal troops toward the defeated population. Felix worked hard in his new and probably not very congenial position to restore civilian confidence and to keep the Union soldiery under control. By this time, he was no longer restrained by inadequate English. He functioned comfortably on his own. The reconstruction of the city was put in hand, and all efforts were made to revive some semblance of normal civilian life. Agnes busied herself with hospital work and there was much to be done. Keeping a sufficient store of supplies took her from time to time to Augusta, or even Nashville, to the Sanitary or Christian Commissions.

Some Atlanta historians consider the Salms the most exotic couple ever to reside in the city, and indeed no other city in the US has ever had a prince in charge. Not much is remembered about what Felix did, except that he was generally well disposed toward the citizenry, but Agnes seems to have made an impact. One historian, Franklin Garrett, notes that she reorganised society as best she could and involved the local ladies in helping her give parties and other entertainment. She mixed with the women of Atlanta in a most friendly fashion, and made a point of joining in their social affairs. A woman of her spontaneous enthusiasm and obvious kindness would have been hard to resist in those grim times.

Garrett goes on,

> Although she defied southern female custom by riding astride, rather than side saddle, she had a southern viewpoint and was sympathetic with the problems of local citizens.

Consequently, she made many friends during the brief time
the General was stationed in Atlanta.[20]

There was some sympathy in the North for the distress of the
destitute white population of Georgia. Well-wishers sent a train to
Atlanta in August laden with clothing and supplies that were con-
fided to Agnes for distribution. Hundreds of poor women flocked
to their house and, reported Agnes, 'I was several days occupied
with this good work. To look on these poor wretched creatures
was a very sad sight. They looked all yellow and starved and were
scarcely covered by rags.' As we have seen elsewhere, Agnes had
a good heart that went out to the unfortunate. She had felt for
the plight of the ruined farmers around Bridgeport, and she was
aghast at the condition to which Sherman had reduced Atlanta
and its citizens. She came from lowly circumstances herself, and
she instinctively sympathised with the downtrodden.

Felix held his post in Atlanta for a scant three months. At the
beginning of October, he and the 68th were ordered to Savannah.
Agnes went to Augusta, where she stayed with the Johnsons.
This is probably when baby Felix was returned to his mother.
Agnes continued her hospital work, visiting Atlanta, Macon and
Nashville, riding on the cow-catcher now and then. 'This manner
of travelling is not at all disagreeable, for one has fresh air, and
is free from the dust and heat of the locomotive.'

She joined Felix in Savannah. The 68th was garrisoned at
nearby Fort Pulaski, where the Salms had very indifferent quarters. Agnes was aghast at the filth, the smell and the damp. The
soldiers came down with cholera and dysentery, and she went back
to Savannah to get provisions, furniture and medical supplies.

Felix managed to get leave, and they went to Augusta by river
steamer, almost sinking in the process. They were in Augusta on
25 October when they learned from Steedman that orders to
disband the 68th had arrived. Sickness had taken its toll and the
regiment was in sorry shape. The Salms returned to Savannah
on 29 November and the 68th was mustered out at Fort Pulaski
the next day. Felix was of a mind to go with the regiment to New
York, but other duties as a brigadier kept him back. Agnes wanted
him to go to Washington with her anyway. They had to think of
the future. Steinhausen was also absent, so Captain Fritsch took
the 68th back to New York by steamer.

Thus, rather anti-climactically, came to an end Prince Felix zu Salm-Salm's service to the Union. He wrote in his memoirs that he was offered a position in the regular army, indeed that 26 senators recommended him, but he did not want to stay in the US. 'I never felt at home in that country, and was horrified at the idea of living a dreary and idle life in some little garrison beyond the pale of civilization.' He had been a soldier since his early youth, he went on to say, and wanted more action.

Then, too, the German-language press in the US had been very hard on him. The fervidly democratic German immigrants were generally intolerant of princes, and Felix had done little to counteract their poor opinion of him and his ways. He had probably had quite enough, and was all too ready to move on to a new environment.

⁂

For someone of Felix's temperament, service with Maximilian, Emperor of Mexico, who was fighting for his existence against the Liberals under Benito Juárez, seemed like a fine idea. A number of American officers were also looking at Mexico as a field for further exploits, but most of them wanted to serve Juárez. Felix went around to see Matias Romero, Juárez's minister in Washington, to bring himself up to date on affairs in that country, but he let on that he was interested in joining the Liberal side.

The next step was to get the necessary letters of introduction to key people in Mexico. These were forthcoming from the Prussian, Austrian and French ministers, the Salms' old friend Gerolt, Baron von Wydenbruck and the Marquis de Montholon. The marquis was important because Maximilian was propped up by the forces of Napoleon III, who had involved him in Mexico in the first place. Agnes's earlier spadework with President Johnson also paid off. 'Even President Johnson, though he could not give him letters of introduction, did not disapprove of it, and on his request gave him a very flattering testimony, in which his services were fully and favourably acknowledged.'

Thus it was that Felix sailed for Veracruz on 24 February 1866, ready to do battle on behalf of Maximilian.

As for Agnes, she too probably found the prospect of adventure in Mexico exciting. A new world to conquer. Despite her long struggle to procure a general's rank for Felix, she certainly had sense enough to know that her man would indeed be happier engaged in deeds of derring-do than facing an uncertain future in the US, which was awash with general officers in the wake of the war. His princely title would count for little in the coming competition for jobs and preferment. She may herself have been uneasy at this uncertain future. A little garrison town out West was definitely not for her either.

They had now been married for almost four years. They had been a good team – Felix eager to find military glory, Agnes eager to see him suitably rewarded and then some even, if the glory was elusive. Had there been ups and downs in their relationship? No doubt, but the relationship was solid. Not all wives would have stuck so close to their husbands and shared their lives as did Agnes in the grim conditions of the Civil War.

She had various matters to attend to, and did not follow until later. She was ready to go on 10 August.

> Driving with Colonel Corvin to the depot and passing the White House, I stopped to say good-bye to the President. He had been very kind to me, and I had seen him frequently. We were admitted at once. Asking him point-blank what he thought of affairs in Mexico, he said that the reign of the Emperor would last still a little while, but he was afraid the United States would have to interfere, though he personally sympathized with Maximilian. He wished me, however, good success, and said that he would always remember me kindly.

She and Jimmy embarked at New York for Havana on board the *Manhattan*, the same ship on which Felix had sailed six months earlier.

PART II

Mexico

6

Maximilian, Emperor of Mexico

Felix's timing was terrible. It was already too late.

The chain of events that brought Archduke Maximilian of Austria to Mexico stretched back half a century or more. Mexico's declaration of independence from Spain in 1821 was the work of conservative elements – the Church, the monastic orders, the military and the landed property owners. Their proclamation declared Mexico a monarchy and guaranteed the Catholic religion and the property and privileges of the Church. Failing a suitable European prince, the Mexican congress elected one Agustín Iturbide as emperor. He lasted less than a year before he was overthrown. Some 40 changes of government followed in the next 35 years as Mexico was pulled back and forth between shifting liberal and conservative factions. One man, Antonio López de Santa Ana, held the presidency eight times and was ousted eight times.

In the midst of all this turmoil came the Mexican–US War of 1846–48 that saw US occupation of Mexico City and ended with the loss of half of Mexico's territory to its relentlessly expanding northern neighbour.

After 1848, with the country's finances in shambles and disorder rampant, Liberals and Conservatives came to form distinct political parties. The Liberals tended to be urban and middle class, and looked to the US as a model of constitutional government. The Conservatives were the party of the religious, military and landed hierarchies; they supported a strong centralised government and looked to the old regimes of Europe for support. Disillusioned by the failure in politic leadership at home, they began to entertain again the idea of a European monarch.

With the final ousting of Santa Ana in 1855, a moderate Liberal government took power and instituted what became known as the Reform. Its principal objectives were to establish a constitutional government with a broad base of support and to destroy the feudal power and privileges of the clergy and the generals. The Reform began as a moderate attempt at change, but was pushed steadily leftward by the fierce hostility of the reactionaries.

Benito Juárez now entered the scene. A Zapotec Indian from Oaxaca, he had had an astonishing rise for one of his background, and in 1855 became minister of justice. The government promulgated laws in 1855 and 1856 that abolished clerical and military privileges and ordered the sale of all Church estates, the aim being to increase government revenues and strengthen the economy. The new federal constitution adopted in February 1857 incorporated the Reform laws and a long list of civil liberties.

The outraged Conservatives mobilised. Pope Pius IX was furious, and the Church excommunicated those who took the oath to the constitution. Isolated reactionary outbreaks coalesced into a major rebellion. Conservative generals seized Mexico City, the government disintegrated and the Reform laws were repealed. Juárez escaped and fled north. The new government in Mexico City sent an army in pursuit, but he eluded them and established his government (Juárez had by now succeeded as Liberal president) at Veracruz on the Caribbean coast. Veracruz was loyal to the constitution, and whoever held the city controlled the customs revenue and the shipment of munitions and other materiel. The terrible three-year War of the Reform had begun.

The European powers supported the Conservative regime; the US favoured the Liberals. The war was vicious and destructive, and in the end, on 11 January 1861, Juárez rode into the capital in his black carriage, the first civilian to govern the country.

In the meantime, Conservative Mexican exiles in Paris and their supporters had gained the ear of Emperor Napoleon III.

They persuaded him that French intervention was necessary to overthrow this Indian radical and restore to Church and aristocracy the properties Juárez had taken from them. Napoleon, who had enjoyed his self-adopted title for barely a decade, saw an opportunity to bolster his sagging popularity at home, win foreign laurels, support the Catholic Church and win a New World empire despite the Anglo-Saxons. The Mexican exiles assured him that the people of Mexico were yearning to be rid of Juárez, and would flock to support a French intervention.

Initially deterred by the uncertainty of what the US might do, Napoleon was given his opportunity by the outbreak of the US Civil War in April 1861. The war also deprived the Mexican Liberals of much-needed support from a generally sympathetic US government.

Mexico was saddled with huge foreign debts, owed principally to Britain and France, and Spain was irritated for various diplomatic reasons and because a number of her citizens had been shot. The Juárez government was destitute, and in July suspended all debt payments for two years. The European powers decided action must be taken, and a joint force landed at Veracruz in December. The French began piling impossible financial demands on the strapped Mexican government. The Spanish and British soon realised they were being used to further French interests, and pulled out in April 1862.

The French moved from the coast to the capital. Despite a stinging setback at Puebla on 5 May 1862, the *Cinco de Mayo* still celebrated as a national holiday in Mexico, they marched into Mexico City on 10 June. Juárez and his cabinet withdrew north to San Luis Potosí.

The Conservative exiles had been pressing for a European prince to rule Mexico, and Napoleon eventually settled on Archduke Maximilian von Habsburg, brother of the Austrian Emperor Franz Joseph. Maximilian, barely 30 years of age, was a gentle innocent of limited experience. He was a handsome man, over six feet tall, with fair skin, blue eyes and blond hair and beard. He had been governor of Lombardy, but his fuzzily liberal (for a Habsburg) ideas had persuaded his brother to remove him before he did too much damage. He was married to Princess Charlotte, daughter of Leopold I of Belgium, a forceful woman who thrilled to the thought of an imperial crown. Franz Joseph was not in the least enthusiastic about the scheme, and he told Maximilian that Austria would in no wise become involved. He warned his brother that he should not accept the offer unless he had firm guarantees of British and French support, and proof positive that the Mexican people would accept him.

The British government saw no possible advantage in supporting Napoleon's dreams of empire. Numerous reports that the Mexicans would resist any foreign intervention such as planned poured in from people who knew Mexico well. The warnings had no effect on the French emperor.

General Achille Bazaine took command of the French forces in July 1863 and moved aggressively to extend French control. By the spring of 1864, Juárez held only the north, while most cities were in French hands. Bazaine was instructed to obtain a favourable plebiscite on Maximilian, and that he did – in the areas the French controlled. A delegation informed the Archduke that the vote had been overwhelmingly in his favour, and in April 1864 he accepted the crown. Napoleon now agreed, in a formal treaty, to keep French troops in Mexico until the end of 1867, while Maximilian undertook to pay not only the costs of the expedition but also the debts due to England, France and Spain. The tragedy was set to open.

Maximilian and Carlota (as the Belgian princess is better known) landed in Veracruz on 28 May 1864. They entered the capital on 12 June. Disillusionment set in almost at once. Maximilian, rather incredibly, wrote to Juárez in Monterrey proposing a meeting to talk over differences. A bitter reply left him in no doubt where the President stood. It gradually became apparent to the imperial pair that, excepting the upper classes in the capital, most of the people did not welcome them. They found the poverty and disorder of the country appalling. The Conservatives, on the other hand, were stunned by the realisation that they had a rather tolerant and liberal man on their hands who had no intention, for example, of restoring the estates and privileges of the clergy. Marshal (as he became in 1864) Bazaine was effectively in charge, and he reported directly to Napoleon, not to Maximilian. The French were detested for their brutality and for their arrogance toward Mexicans of all classes. The state had little money, yet the imperial pair spent recklessly on balls and entertainments and on redecorating the old palace of Chapultepec on the hill to the west of the city. Poor Maximilian seems genuinely to have loved Mexico and those Mexicans he managed to meet, and he did want to help the poor and deprived, but the impossibility of his situation, both in Mexico and internationally, seems not to have penetrated his conscience.

Bazaine advanced on all fronts in 1864. In the south the stronghold of Oaxaca was taken, and in the north Juárez was driven against the US border. Pockets of resistance remained in the mountainous districts, but most of Mexico lay sullenly under French occupation.

By the time the Salms arrived in the summer of 1866, the situation had changed radically, and for the worse. Military campaigns had degenerated into savage guerrilla warfare and both sides executed prisoners without ceremony. The American Civil War had ended more than a year earlier, thus allowing the US, with its self-confidence more than restored, to pay attention once more to Mexico. Secretary of State William Seward now pressed Napoleon to withdraw from Mexico. Arms and munitions began to flow to the Juaristas. The French public opposed the whole imperial scheme and its huge expense. A restless Prussia under Bismarck was beginning to make dangerous noises. Napoleon found himself in an increasingly difficult situation. Bazaine was ordered to withdraw, and it was hoped that Maximilian would go with him. The withdrawal began in March 1866. As the French withdrew, the Juaristas advanced into the vacuum. The north was quickly overrun, and in October 1866 Oaxaca fell to Porfirio Díaz, the future long-term president and dictator.

Maximilian was thunderstruck. Napoleon had pledged him his support, and now this? Envoys were sent to Paris; no help was forthcoming. By July, the possibility of abdication began to be considered. After all, the French had been scheduled all along to depart by the end of 1867, and it looked increasingly unlikely that they would hang on that long. Carlota refused to countenance the idea of a Habsburg abdicating, and in August she left for Europe on a desperate search for help, in the course of which her mind gave way. The empire had shrunk to little more than Mexico City and nearby Puebla, Querétaro to the north and Veracruz on the coast.

⁂

Felix arrived in Veracruz in July 1866 and made his way to the capital. He had letters of introduction from Gerolt, the Prussian minister in Washington, and the Austrian and French ministers there to the Prussian minister in Mexico, Baron Anton von Magnus, Count Thun, the Austrian minister, and Marshal Bazaine. The plan was for Thun to introduce Felix to the Emperor, but that gentleman did everything he could to thwart him and to prevent him getting an army appointment. Prussia had just trounced Austria in the Seven Weeks' War (June–August 1866), and Count Thun was in no mood to do favours for a Prussian prince. He was soon replaced by Baron von Lago, but he was not very helpful either. Magnus, on the other hand, was helpful. Felix was appointed a colonel and assigned to the staff of one of the French generals.

Agnes reached Havana on 13 August. She was thrilled to find Felix there to meet her. He had been laid low in Veracruz with a bout of malaria, but managed to recover sufficiently to get to his beloved wife. He brought the sad news that 'Old Groeben', their faithful major domo during the Civil War years, had died. Groeben had brewed up many a whisky punch for them and their guests at their camps during the war, and had accompanied Agnes on many of her expeditions.

They sailed for Veracruz, and on 25 August began their journey to the capital, some 400 miles away. The first leg of the trip was by train across the hot, steamy coastal plain to Paso del Macho, where they transferred to a coach drawn by eight mules for the long hard climb up the mountains to the highlands of central Mexico, some 7000 feet above them. As they reached more temperate climes, Agnes's spirits improved, and she describes the lovely countryside with its cultivated fields and farms and the profusion of beautiful flowers. From time to time, they and the other two passengers descended from the coach and walked to take some of the load off the struggling mules and to escape the terrible jolting.

The carriage broke down on the second day, and they were offered shelter in a nearby Indian hut. This was Agnes's first close look at the people over whose heads most of Mexican politics boiled. She was struck by the cleanliness of the simple hut, by the courtesy and kindness of the Indian couple and by their close family life. But she remarked on their 'submissive manners and melancholy air of resignation always to be seen in nations subjugated and ill-treated by barbarians for centuries, for such were the Christian Spaniards who conquered Mexico'. She thought the Indians more interesting than the descendants of their conquerors. All they needed, she said, was an enlightened and firm government, but since that would never be provided by the white or Indian Mexicans themselves, she hoped the US would take over the country! She castigated the Spanish for debasing the Indians. 'If the Aztec priests were cruel, they were no more so than the Christian priests who punished them barbarically for their errors instead of teaching the religion of love.' Agnes did have her compassionate side when she saw injustice and poverty.

The horizon was now dominated by the awesome peak of Orizaba, at over 18,000 feet the highest mountain in Mexico. They left the town of Orizaba at five in the morning for Puebla, and now the other two great volcanic peaks of Popocatepetl and Iztaccihuatl loomed above them. Agnes liked the old colonial town of Puebla, where they rested for two days before the final lap of their journey. Felix was happy running into some Austrian officers whom he knew.

The last day took them yet further upward through the great pine forests that cloak the mountains surrounding the Valley of Mexico. And finally, there was the city below them – the lakes shining in the sun, the palaces and gardens, the great cathedral in the centre, all glistening beneath a pure blue sky in the crystalline air that is, alas, but a distant memory now. They were enchanted.

They settled down and embarked on a busy round of social affairs, meeting the city's leading lights. They saw a good deal of Baron Magnus, who was to play a leading role in their lives in the months ahead. Agnes had nothing good whatsoever to say about Bazaine and the French, who treated the Mexicans with 'the utmost arrogance and contempt'. She wrote of their insatiable greed and their offensiveness to Mexicans of both sexes. 'Bazaine,' she observed, 'behaved there as if he was the Emperor and Maximilian his subordinate... He was not only arrogant, brutal and cruel, he was also rapacious and mean, and employed the lowest artifices to enrich himself.'

She liked the people of the capital and described the dress and habits and daily lives of the different classes – the *criollos*, Mexican-born but of Spanish descent, the Spanish-Indian *mestizos*, and of course the Indians. The typical houses with their interior courts and galleries she found attractive. She was impressed by the horses, intelligent and strong. The men she found polite and courteous, but they were not reliable, she thought. Good at words, but not at the follow-through. The ladies were very pretty and good mothers, but they were remarkably ignorant, reading nothing but their prayer books. But then, she wrote, 'Fifty years of civil war would demoralise better nations than the descendants of Cortez's rapacious crew'. She did her homework and gave a reasonably accurate account of Mexico's history and the conquest. She thought the Spanish had behaved barbarously, and she repeatedly expressed her sympathy for the lot of the Indians.

Ladies did not usually walk abroad, except to go to church and their morning stroll in the Alameda, the park in the centre of town. That would certainly not do for Agnes, and she spent happy hours exploring the markets, where she was delighted with all the different and unfamiliar products and the beautiful flowers.

In the capital were Austrian and Belgian troops among whom were many titled officers, Felix's type of society, and they spent most of their social life with them. Agnes's forays into local colour did not attract Felix. Excursions to the country were popular, though they had to keep an eye out for bands of Liberals. Life was agreeable, and though the difficult political situation must have weighed on them, it receives no mention.

Agnes could always be counted upon to embrace a high-level plot. Magnus, fresh from an interview with Maximilian, called on her one day with a fantastic scheme that involved nothing less than persuading the US Congress, sceptical about a monarchy next door, to recognise Maximilian's government. Agnes was, as usual, convinced of her special talents.

> This [US recognition] would have been of the highest importance, and increased the chance of Maximilian's success more than the ambiguous and humiliating patronage of the French emperor…As I was well acquainted not only with President Johnson and most of the influential persons in the United States, but also with the best ways and means in which to work upon them, Baron Magnus had suggested to the Emperor the idea of sending me to Washington on a secret diplomatic mission, accompanied by a most powerful ally – two millions of dollars in gold.

One does not quite know what to make of this story. It seems rather improbable, but Magnus must have had something in mind. Agnes was thrilled to be at the centre of such a mission, of course, and she was all set to go, but Felix refused to let her make the trip alone and insisted on accompanying her. They must have had something of a row, and Agnes sniffed, 'He had very little diplomatic talent, and did not understand how to deal with Americans as I did. I knew that he would rather render my task more difficult, but as he obstinately insisted, I could not refuse him.'

The matter was set for discussion at a dinner with the Emperor at Chapultepec Palace. But plans for the dinner party, and in consequence the whole scheme, suddenly collapsed. Maximilian received news from Europe of his wife's mental illness, and he left the capital on 21 October for Orizaba, where he had a favourite hacienda.

There was more to it than that. On learning of Carlota's breakdown, Maximilian wanted to go to her, but the situation in Mexico was too grave. Napoleon, desperate for an easy way out, urged abdication. Bazaine received instructions to open negotiations with certain of the Liberal generals. Maximilian drafted an abdication proclamation and withdrew to Orizaba, where his Conservative ministers and the clerical party, whose lives and futures were at stake, urged him to stay. His leading generals, Miguel Miramón and Leonardo Márquez, joined the chorus. And from Vienna came a letter from his mother, Archduchess

Sophie, a woman of considerable strength of character, telling him to do his duty and stand fast.

Maximilian placed the issue before his cabinet. The majority voted for him to stay, so he returned to Mexico City and prepared to fight. He was now completely in the hands of the Conservative faction, whose more extreme policies he had, in fact, resisted for so long. Outside these circles, the empire was widely perceived as being doomed. Marshal Bazaine began to treat directly with the Juarista generals through whose territory he would have to withdraw his troops to the port of Veracruz.

While all this was going on, the Salms amused themselves in Mexico City. 'The life we were leading was pleasant enough,' wrote Agnes, 'but my Hotspur Felix panted for war. Though as kind-hearted as could be, and gentle as a lamb, he had the pugnacious instincts of a fighting cock. War was his very element.' Other than summing up neatly Felix's chief characteristic, this remark again raises the question of Agnes's education. Comparing Felix rather aptly to Sir Henry Percy (d.1403), the fiery-tempered warrior son of the first earl of Northumberland, indicates that Agnes knew her history or her Shakespeare (*Henry IV* Part 1) or both. The comparison was more apt than she knew: both Hotspurs met the same fate.

At length Felix managed to obtain permission to join a reconnaissance expedition under the commanding officer of the Belgian force in Mexico, Colonel Alfred van der Smissen. Agnes insisted on going along, and after much argument the men relented. She could not resist a smart military uniform, and she had run up for herself a costume in the silver and gray of the Belgian regiment. The refined ladies of Mexico City's society were scandalised by Agnes's interest in military matters, and in sharing the hardships of army life with her husband, but Agnes could not have cared less.

The Belgian party was at Teotihuacan when the colonel received orders on 1 January 1867 to proceed at once to Buena Vista, a village between Puebla and the capital, where Maximilian was due to stop en route back to the capital. Thus it was that the Salms watched the Emperor arrive in a small carriage drawn by four white mules. He appeared very drawn. Colonel van der

Smissen remarked to Agnes that he looked as though he were being led to his execution.

On 5 February 1867 Bazaine and the French forces marched out of Mexico City heading for the coast and home. The crowd watched in silence. Agnes and Felix stood behind a palace window on the Plaza Mayor as the troops passed below. Maximilian did not appear. The Emperor now stood alone with his Mexicans and a few contingents of Austrians and Belgians. The Austrian and Belgian units had been summoned home by their governments, but a number of officers and men signed on with the Mexican army and stayed behind to support the imperial cause.

7

Querétaro

Eight days later, Maximilian left Mexico City for Querétaro with General Márquez and a troop of 2000 cavalry. Why he went to Querétaro, a sixteenth-century colonial town 140 miles northeast of Mexico City in enemy-controlled territory, already threatened by two Liberal generals, lying in a plain surrounded by hills and thus difficult to defend, has long been debated. Even Felix wrote, during the siege that was to follow, 'To permit the enemy to shut us up in a place situated so unfavourably as Queretaro, which had neither a political nor strategical importance, seemed to me not only ridiculous but even fatal'.[1]

In addition to its natural weakness, the town had not been provisioned to handle the increased number of troops and the rigours of a siege. Food, water and ammunition were in short supply from the very beginning. It was, however, loyal to the imperial cause and free from the intrigues of the capital, where the ultra-Conservatives held sway.

Maximilian had determined to take no European officers with him, only loyal Mexicans. Felix would have none of that. He was beside himself when he learned that he would be left behind. He had come to Mexico for the express purpose of fighting – here at last was the prospect of serious action and he was not going to idle away his time in Mexico City! He ran at once to Magnus, but not even he could persuade the Emperor to change his mind and 'satisfy the pugnacious longings of my impetuous

Felix,' as Agnes put it. At last, General Santiago Vidaurri, one of the oldest of the Conservative generals, agreed that Felix could join his staff. The Secretary of War signed off on the plan and Felix was all set to go. For once, he seems to have managed all this on his own, with Magnus's help but not that of Agnes.

Maximilian was rather startled when he spotted Felix among the troops, but he raised no objection and said he was glad to see him. They started at once, the Emperor riding at the head of his troops. As the column reached the top of the pass, Maximilian must have turned and looked back on the city below him, and wondered. Then he faced north and struck out along the valleys winding through the mountains to Querétaro.

On 19 February the imperial party reached the top of Cuesta China, the principal hill overlooking Querétaro. As they entered the city, they were greeted by Generals Miramón and Mejía, who had arrived earlier with 3000 men. The civilian population greeted them warmly. The following day, General Méndez arrived with another 4000 men, bringing the total of the imperial forces in the city to 9000. The cast was assembled for the final act of the drama. Of the principal players, the two most influential were Miramón and Márquez.

Miguel Miramón (1831–67) had been the leading Conservative commander during the War of the Reform. For a brief spell in 1859–60 he held the presidency of the reactionary regime based in Mexico City, in opposition to Juárez. Following the Liberal victory, he went to Europe, where he joined those advocating foreign intervention and promoting Maximilian's candidacy for the throne. He returned as a partisan of the Emperor. Maximilian did not particularly care for his brand of conservatism, however, and in 1864 packed him off to Berlin to study artillery. He returned in 1866, and early in 1867, in a daring raid, came within an ace of capturing Juárez at Zacatecas in the north. He was known for his aggressive tactics.

Leonardo Márquez (1820–1913) was a far darker character. He had fought on the Conservative side during the civil war at the end of which he took refuge in the Sierra Gorda near Querétaro. He joined the French in 1862 and fought under Bazaine, gaining a well-deserved reputation for cruelty. As one historian has remarked, 'Few generals, even in Mexico, have devoted themselves more whole-heartedly to the shooting of prisoners and the murdering of political opponents'.[2] During the presidency of Miramón, Márquez won a resounding victory over the Liberals at Tacubaya, not far from the capital. A number of prisoners were taken. Miramón gave orders that the captured officers should be executed, whereupon Márquez simply shot all the prisoners plus a number of medical students who had come out from the capital to care for the wounded. He was henceforth known as the 'Tiger of Tacubaya'. Maximilian did not entirely care for him either, and sent him to Constantinople as envoy in 1864. He too returned in 1866. Why this man later, in the dark days of Querétaro, should have held such a fascination for kindly Maximilian is something of a mystery, but defer to his judgments he did.

Tomás Mejía (1820–67) was a short, dark Otomí Indian who had also fought under Bazaine and had a record of success against the Juaristas. The mountains around Querétaro were the home of his people. His men worshipped him. He was a staunch defender of the Church, and viewed the struggle against the Liberals as something of a crusade. He was famous for his terrifying cavalry charges. In 1856 he had raised his people against the Reform laws and had seized Querétaro.

Ramón Méndez was also of Indian stock. He had the blood of a couple of Liberal generals on his hands, executed after being defeated.

Santiago Vidaurri, the oldest of the lot, had controlled the northern province of Nuevo León since well before the War of the Reform. He had originally supported – from a distance – Juárez, but when the French began to press his domains in 1864, he went over to them. He finally opted for Maximilian.

Approaching Querétaro from San Luis Potosí to the north was the Juarista General Mariano Escobedo. Miramón pressed for an immediate attack, carrying the battle to the enemy while they were still on the move, but Márquez urged restraint: let them concentrate their forces so they can be hit all at once. While the imperial generals argued strategy, on 6 March Escobedo joined up with a second army coming from the southwest, and stood with 35,000 men and siege artillery before Querétaro.

Felix wrote of the siege in great detail. He gloried in being back in the kind of action he loved. He was devoted to the Emperor, and usually sided with the aggressive and action-prone Miramón against the more cautious Márquez.

The Emperor originally had his headquarters on the Cerro de las Campañas, or Hill of Bells, dominating the western side of the town. Under constant attack and bombardment, and with the main body of the enemy massing north and west of town, Maximilian was persuaded to move his command post to the Convento de la Santa Cruz at the eastern end of town. This splendid building, a natural fortress, massed around its courtyard, was built in 1654, about a century after the Spanish had founded Querétaro. The next day Escobedo attacked in force and was beaten off with heavy losses. Felix was in the thick of the fight.

He was with Maximilian on 2 March when a dispatch arrived from Mexico with the news that his ministers would not send troops, fearing for their own skins and not wanting to endanger the capital. They stood alone.

Felix had no special duties until the Emperor offered him command of the Cazadores, a select corps requiring, he wrote, great energy to command. They hailed him warmly. The corps consisted of nearly 700 men, mostly French, but there were also Germans, Hungarians and about 150 Mexicans. It was a wild bunch of the bravest soldiers that could be found, wrote Felix. When they were not actually in combat, they fought among themselves, and Felix had his hands full preventing 'bloodshed and murder', but as soon as they charged against the enemy, they were like one man.

One of his subordinates in the Cazadores was Major Ernst Pitner, who had arrived in Mexico in early 1865 as a lieutenant with an Austrian volunteer unit. He saw action in various parts of the country, and in June 1866 was taken captive with his unit in a battle with a Liberal army under Escobedo near the mouth of the Rio Grande. Escobedo released him in February 1867 on the condition that he head for Veracruz and leave for Europe, but when he reached Querétaro – which he too saw as difficult to defend – and saw how few European officers Maximilian had, he offered his services. Márquez took him on as a major and put him in the Cazadores. Pitner left a valuable diary of his experiences in Mexico.

Another participant in the siege who left a written record was Albert Hans, a lieutenant of artillery, who served under Méndez. Hans too was a passionate defender of the imperial cause. He prefaced his account of the siege, published in 1869, with an open letter to Empress Carlota, which, if that unhappy lady ever read it, might have given her some small solace. Hans described Felix as 'a superior officer, whose monocle, moustache and Germanic character reveal a true Prussian'.[3]

Lt Hans remarked that Felix's Cazadores were made up largely of the debris of former French and Mexican battalions, but he knew how to handle them very well – like Prussians.

> Prince Salm, who had taken command of the Franco-Mexican chasseurs, was charged with seizing [an enemy battery] with his battalion … The chasseurs, Prince Salm at their head, threw themselves into the attack, cleared the bridge under enemy fire, put to flight all those they encountered as well as the defenders of the battery, and took the gun.[4]

Felix wrote that they overwhelmed the enemy post with a loss of 30 dead and wounded to the enemy's 300. This was all very well, but the enemy had men to spare.

Three days later, in another foray, Felix distinguished himself again. He owed his life only to his horse shying and throwing up its head, thus taking in its own skull a musket ball that would otherwise have hit his master.

At a staff meeting on 15 March, Miramón and Felix again counselled attack, building on the success of the previous day when the defenders had thrown the enemy back. But again Márquez urged restraint. 'The Emperor,' wrote Felix, 'was perfectly infatuated with Marquez. Though a man of good sense, his character was too noble and too pure to suspect the honesty of others. A Napoleon and a Marquez had easy work with a nature like his.' Márquez carried his point, and it was decided to remain in Querétaro.

In Pitner's opinion, the Emperor was a poor judge of character, generally ill-served by those he trusted. He was also fatally indecisive. He was fond of calling staff meetings to discuss issues he himself was incapable of resolving, but lacking any forceful leadership from the supposed commander-in-chief, the meetings were marked by disunity and indecision that only inhibited the effective use of the forces available. Márquez so consistently opposed any forward strategy that Pitner wondered if he was not being deliberately obstructionist.

Felix moved another notch up on 20 March when the Emperor gave him command of the 1st Brigade in Méndez's division. Pitner took command of the Cazadores.

Reinforcements were absolutely necessary if they were to hold out. It was decided to send Márquez and Vidaurri to Mexico City to raise troops and get money. Under cover of an attack on the besiegers launched by Miramón, in which Felix and his Cazadores played a significant role, the two generals slipped out on 22 March and reached the capital. Márquez did manage to round up a force of sorts, and even to get his hands on some money, but then he made a grave miscalculation. Porfirio Díaz was moving on the capital from the south, and on 2 April seized Puebla. Faced with this immediate threat, Márquez decided to defend Mexico City rather than lead his newly gathered army back to Querétaro. The two armies clashed on 10 April, and the imperialists were routed. Márquez fell back on Mexico City and prepared to hold it. Díaz, wasting no time, captured Chapultepec and Maximilian's palace.

Meanwhile, the defenders of Querétaro waited in vain for the reinforcements. The attacks continued, as did the almost daily bombardments. Felix reported a terrific attack of some 6000 of the enemy on 24 March; the besieged triumphed, but it was costly in terms of men and munitions. He still wore his monocle; he reports it being covered with dust after a shell exploded, and not being able to see as he tried to extricate himself from the wrecked building.

And so it went. The besieged won occasional victories and were cheered, but inexorably the vice was closing. It became harder and harder to slip through enemy lines, even in the rugged terrain around the city. Felix commented on Maximilian's frequent visits to the trenches and the hospitals, how kind he was, and how the men responded.

Maximilian never overlooked an opportunity for ceremony. On 30 March he bestowed decorations. The generals – Miramón, Mejía, Méndez and three others – were lined up in the front rank, and the Emperor ordered Felix to join them. About this time Maximilian told him that he wanted to make him a general, but he feared the reaction from the Mexicans. For jealousy there was, but Felix made a point of mentioning those – including the three generals named above – who did not, apparently, resent the partiality the Emperor showed him. For by now, he had become the Emperor's closest companion, not surprising given that he was the highest-ranking European around and, more-over, a German prince.

Count Corti, author of an early book on Maximilian and Carlota, remembered fellow Austrians who felt that in these dire days Felix did not have sufficient experience or, for that matter, regard for the future to impress upon Maximilian the true gravity of the situation. Nonetheless,

> The Emperor's 'latest adviser', as he was distrustfully called in the imperial army, though essentially an adventurer, was a brave and trusty man. His courageous devotion had stood every test brilliantly. Maximilian, who had a fine appreciation of true personal loyalty, became a true friend of the Prince during the last weeks of his life.[5]

Another council of war met on 2 April. With the exception of Miramón, who argued that Querétaro could be held indefinitely, the generals urged that Maximilian break out with the cavalry and head northeast to the rugged Sierra Gorda, Mejía's country, which already sheltered an imperialist force of some 1000 men. But Maximilian refused: it was against his honour to abandon the army and, besides, reported Felix, he could not believe that Márquez would not return. In this debate, Felix sided with Miramón and did his utmost to stiffen the Emperor's resolve.

Maximilian had a highly developed if possibly misdirected sense of obligation and duty. He had been elected to the throne of Mexico (though by this time even he must have realised the election was suspect), and he was going to see the job through. He was also loyal to his subordinates and those who depended upon him, and he would not let them down.

The day set for the return of Márquez, 5 April, came and went, with no word. Scouts were sent out to secure information, but most were captured and strung up. None returned.

Fissures in the command structure became ever more apparent. Miramón and Méndez quarrelled incessantly. The latter took Felix aside at one point and told him to tell the Emperor

> to try to get out as fast as possible from this mousetrap, and to beware of Miramón. I am an Indian, and the Emperor knows the faithfulness and the devotion of the Indians for him. If he orders, I will arrest Miramón. Mejía and myself will bring the Emperor in safety to the Sierra Gorda…Should he not follow this advice, he may depend on it that we shall all be shot.

When Felix passed this message along, the Emperor responded, 'The little stout one takes too gloomy a view of our matters, although I believe he means well'. Besides, Maximilian was determined not to take flight, leaving behind his army and the people of Querétaro who had stood by him so staunchly. It seems most likely that the well-meaning Emperor knew at the bottom of his heart that the game was up, but he was a Habsburg through and through, and a Habsburg did not desert his post. Even his mother had told him so.

Miramón, aggressive as usual and frustrated by confinement, launched a major attack on 11 April to the east of Santa Cruz along the eighteenth-century aqueduct. Felix had warned Miramón that the plan would not work, and he was much discomfited not only by being obliged to fall back, but by nearly being killed by rifle fire. He complained to Maximilian about the general's alleged shortcomings, but the Emperor waved them off. Lt Hans described Felix's near miss.

> Prince Salm was saved by a young Frenchman, a sub-lieutenant of the chasseurs, who, spotting the barrel of a gun protruding from a loophole and aimed at the prince, gave him a vigorous shove. He fell an instant before the gun fired. Otherwise he would have been hit point blank.[6]

Pitner was wounded in the action.

On the fifteenth, the Emperor decided to send Felix with cavalry to Mexico City to find Márquez and bring him back. He even authorised him to arrest Márquez if necessary. Miramón had to be consulted, and Felix was enraged when the general insisted that his friend General Moret go with him. Felix believed Moret woefully unqualified for the tricky assignment, but Miramón prevailed, and in the end a joint command was arranged, much to Felix's chagrin. Maximilian gave him a long list of instructions about contacting foreign diplomats and the press, getting money and above all reinforcements, but the principal object of the foray was to come back with Márquez's cavalry.

The party set off on the night of the eighteenth from the Cerro de las Campañas, but when they reached the little Río Blanca a superior force of enemy infantry suddenly appeared from behind the hills on the far side. Moret proved his incompetence by abruptly falling back. Felix was convinced they had been betrayed. He suspected Colonel Miguel López, whom he had long mistrusted but who had the confidence of the Emperor. The Emperor, Felix groused, was prone to telling López things better kept confidential. Increasingly aware of the difficulty of his position, the Emperor now refused to let Felix try again to reach Mexico City, and appointed him first aide-de-camp.

From among the Germans in the ranks, Felix had acquired a servant named Muth. Frustrated in his own attempt to get out and collect intelligence, he tried to send Muth to Mexico City on the twentieth, but the man was captured before he could get very far. Loyal to his prince and emperor, the resourceful spy pretended to be a deserter. He found out what he could in the enemy camp and then escaped to return to Querétaro. He brought the terrible news of Márquez's defeat by Díaz two weeks previously.

The Emperor was finally moved to action, and resolved to break out, with the army. Only Miramón, Felix and General Severo Castillo were privy to the plan. They spent the twenty-sixth preparing. Felix was appointed chief of the imperial household, such as it was. To cover up their movements, Miramón and Castillo launched a major attack on the twenty-seventh. It was a success, and the Liberals fell back. If Miramón had followed it up at once, Felix wrote, perhaps optimistically, the situation might have been turned to their favour, but Miramón wasted precious time urging the Emperor to postpone leaving Querétaro in favour of another massive attack to annihilate the enemy. The delay allowed Escobedo to regroup and the Liberals quickly recovered lost ground. The imperial troops were routed. The Emperor changed his mind again.

Begging the Emperor's pardon for speaking so bluntly, Felix strongly advised him to leave. 'But all in vain. The Emperor was utterly infatuated with Miramón. He spoke again of his "military honour" which would not permit him to give up the city with all its heavy artillery.' And the poor people of Querétaro who had suffered so much for his sake – how could he abandon them, or the wounded? 'Thus ended the 27th of April, which offered us the last chance of safety.'

By 1 May the imperial forces had been locked up in Querétaro for more than three weeks. It had been six weeks since their arrival in the city. They were under incessant bombardment. They were critically short of supplies. The defenders had dwindled through losses and desertion to some 7000 men. A council of war on 11 May decided, again, on a breakout with the whole army. Even Felix joined the chorus urging Maximilian to make a dash for safety. To cover their movements and create a diversion, General Mejía organised and armed 3000 local Indians to occupy the imperial lines while the defenders evacuated. The Emperor told Felix he wanted to promote him to general, but this was not to be announced until they had all left Querétaro. Maximilian wanted to reward his faithful friend and companion, but not at the expense of annoying the Mexican officers on whom his safety depended.

On the evening of the fourteenth, everything was set to go. Felix worked till after midnight arranging Maximilian's papers for travel. But now, once again, the Emperor delayed matters, for 24 hours. In the early hours of 15 May a Liberal force gained access to the garden of the Convento de Santa Cruz and swiftly overcame the exhausted garrison. At four in the morning of the fifteenth, Maximilian was awakened with the news that the enemy was already in the convent. He dressed and with his private secretary, José Luis Blasio, Felix and several officers descended to the courtyard of the convent. Incredibly, none of the milling Liberal soldiers recognised him, and he was able to mount his horse and, with his small group of followers, ride the length of town to the Cerro de las Campañas, where he surrendered.

Many have long believed that Colonel Miguel López was bribed to admit the Liberals at the sector he commanded. López commanded the 'Empress' Regiment at Chapultepec, and was in charge of security at Santa Cruz. He had escorted Maximilian and Carlota from Veracruz to the capital when they first arrived in Mexico, and Maximilian had always treated him kindly. He was godfather to one of his children. Felix had always suspected his loyalty, and was convinced of his treachery, as were Basch and Blasio, but a number of historians are not so sure.

In a letter of 1887 to Porfirio Díaz, then president of Mexico, Escobedo stated flatly that López was not a traitor. From early April, wrote the retired general, exhausted and demoralised deserters of all ranks had made it out of the beleaguered city to Liberal lines. Maximilian's troops were in very poor shape, low in both discipline and morale. The foreign troops were trapped in an impossible situation, and Escobedo was fully aware of the quarrels among the defending generals. It was only a matter of time.

On 14 May, he wrote, Colonel López appeared in his camp, sent secretly by Maximilian to ask for a meeting to avoid further bloodshed. He would abandon Querétaro, López reported, if Escobedo would grant him and his household free passage to Veracruz, where he would embark for Europe. Escobedo told López that Maximilian must give his word of honour to quit Mexico and never return. He then sent López back to Maximilian with the message that at 3.00 a.m. Santa Cruz would be occupied, resistance or no. And so it was done. Knowing the true state of affairs in the city, Escobedo had simply taken advantage of the Emperor's desperate situation to make his move.[7]

Even this testimony does not convince the anti-López camp, and the debate continues. But if Escobedo's account is to be believed, Maximilian was perhaps more aware of his plight than Felix and many others thought at the time. Felix had complained that Maximilian took López too much into his confidence, and it is possible that the unhappy Emperor felt that a Mexican emissary to the Mexican general might accomplish more than all the brave schemes of Felix and his generals. In any case, it is also significant that the Liberals did not arrest López. Felix and others took this as proof of his treachery; it may instead have been a reward for his efforts as a go-between.

Returning to the Cerro de las Campañas the morning of 15 May, Maximilian wanted to go down fighting, but his generals persuaded him that resistance was hopeless and he should surrender. This he did, to the first officer he encountered as he descended the hill, giving up his sword. The party was escorted to Escobedo. Felix reported the scene.

> Escobedo invited the Emperor to enter a tent standing there and I followed, as Escobedo had also an officer with him... Besides us four, nobody was a witness to the conversation ensuing. After the Emperor had been standing a few minutes before Escobedo and the latter remained silent, the Emperor said: 'If more blood must be spilled, take only mine.' This and two other requests were made by the Emperor; first, to spare his army; and secondly, to enable all persons belonging to his house, and who wished it, to get to the coast, for the purpose of embarking for Europe.

Escobedo replied that he would report these requests to his superiors, and that the Emperor and his followers would be treated as prisoners of war.

Thus it was that the Emperor, a dozen generals, 20 colonels, 375 other officers and upwards of 7000 rank and file passed into captivity.

Maximilian was taken back to Santa Cruz, where Escobedo visited him the next morning, he being too ill with dysentery to move. He asked Maximilian, now generally referred to by the more polite Liberals as the Archduke, if he wished any of his followers to be incarcerated with him, and he chose Felix, José Luis Blasio, his personal physician Dr Basch and two others. They were confined in Santa Cruz, 400 other officers in a church. Maximilian's dysentery did not abate, and Dr Basch was able to consult with the chief surgeon of the Liberal forces, on whose recommendations he was moved first to the Teresita Convent and then to the Convent of the Capuchins, where conditions were better. Through the good offices of Carlos Rubio, a local merchant, the prisoners were reasonably well provisioned.

Escobedo ordered that any officer who did not surrender at once would be executed. Méndez, who feared retaliation for past brutalities, had gone into hiding. He was found, and on 19 May shot. For the rest, their ordeal was just beginning.

Blasio described the disposition of the prisoners. While the Emperor was taken to Santa Cruz,

> We were more than 600 prisoners in the church, some sitting on the altars, others in the confessionals and on the benches, telling each other of their various adventures. Many were smoking, and one of the smokers distractedly threw his cigar butt into a cartridge box full of cartridges that was on the floor. There was a tremendous explosion and a terrible panic swept through the crowd. The guards at the door of the church, seeing the prisoners running for the exit, fired into the throng, killing some unfortunates and wounding others.[8]

Meanwhile, what of Agnes during these long lonely weeks?

8

Agnes Goes on the Offensive

Agnes had a terrific tantrum when Felix left her behind in Mexico City and marched off to Querétaro.

> I of course expected to go with Salm as usual, but for once, he refused in a most determined manner and remained deaf to all my entreaties. Now it was my turn to become mad. I cried and screamed so as to be heard two blocks off; and Jimmy, who felt for his mistress, howled and barked; but Salm stole away and took a street where he could not hear me and I not see him. I believe I hated him at that moment, and felt very unhappy, for I knew he would come to grief, having never had any luck without me.

That last remark speaks volumes.

She soon recovered her equilibrium, however, and grudgingly admitted that perhaps Felix had been thinking of her safety and comfort. He had arranged for her to stay with a family named Hube at their large and comfortable house in Tacubaya, just south of Chapultepec. Mr Hube had been Mexican consul-general in Hamburg. He and his wife were most kind to Agnes, and she invariably spoke very highly of them.

For weeks nothing was heard from Querétaro but vague and contradictory reports. At last General Márquez arrived with 3000 men, causing great excitement in the city. Agnes was extremely anxious for news of Felix, so she asked Hube to go with her to see Márquez.

The general received them graciously, but Agnes was irritated by his airs and self-importance. He spoke as though the Emperor was his pupil, and he was condescending to her. He had high words of praise for Felix, though, and told Agnes of his exploits and bravery. Agnes and Hube then went to call on General Vidaurri, who echoed Márquez's optimistic picture of the situation in Querétaro and also heaped praise on Felix.

The good news was, of course, quite false, but everyone was elated and there was much celebrating. Meanwhile, the Liberal General Porfirio Díaz was advancing on Puebla. Márquez prepared to attack, on, he maintained, the Emperor's orders, but this too was false. He marched out, leaving behind only a small garrison that was not enough to deter Liberal guerrillas from infiltrating the outskirts of the city. There was fighting around Tacubaya.

News trickled back of a great victory, but on the fourth day the truth became known: Márquez had been defeated decisively and Díaz was advancing. Márquez and what was left of his army got back into the city, and were able to prevent the Liberals from entering the capital proper, but Díaz did take Tacubaya and then Chapultepec.

Agnes was true to form.

> The advanced guard of the Liberal army passed our house in Tacubaya, and I admired their fine horses and uniforms, the greater part of which they had taken from the Imperialists. Before their arrival, fighting between the Imperialists and Liberal guerillas was going on in the very streets of Tacubaya, and frequently right before our house. Though we had closed the blind my curiosity prevailed, and I and Helena Hube [the daughter] peeped out to see what was going on, to the dismay of old Mr. Hube, who was afraid a bullet might kill or wound us. The spectacle was, however, too attractive, and we could not stay away.

By now the true state of affairs in the besieged city had become known. The grim news spurred Agnes on. Her man needed her, and so did the unfortunate Emperor. She was determined to save them, and she had to get to Porfirio Díaz at Chapultepec. Hube was flatly opposed to her plans, and went so far as to lock her in the house. She waited till dawn, when the servants came, and persuaded them to let her out. Faced with the Agnes brand of determination, Hube finally let her go. With no transportation available, she had to walk, Margarita the maid and the faithful Jimmy trailing behind. The maid was in absolute terror, since the place was overrun with Liberal soldiers, but Hube was known to have Liberal sympathies, and Agnes's association with him helped. It must have been at least two miles to Chapultepec, and then they had to climb the steep outcrop on which the castle sits.

Once there, she asked for Colonel León, a Liberal officer whom she knew and who had spent two years in the US. She told him she had to get to the capital to try to save the Emperor and her husband. Her aims were breathtaking. She wanted to talk to the commanders of the foreign troops in Mexico City to ascertain if they would surrender if Díaz would guarantee the lives and liberty of the Emperor and his officers should they fall into Liberal hands. This was the old Agnes back at work: never waste time with underlings, go straight to the top.

The Colonel, no doubt staggered by this determined young lady, escorted her towards the outposts defending the capital. She marched across the fields toward the line of defences. The imperial officers commanding recognised her, and she had no difficulties. The soldiers very politely laid boards across the ditch and helped her over the ramparts.

She sought out Baron Magnus, the Prussian minister, who took her to see two of the foreign commanders, Austrians, with whom Colonel León had agreed to talk. Given the uncertainty of the situation, the lack of reliable news from Querétaro and no authorisation from the Emperor, the two Austrians were unwilling to initiate negotiations. Their reluctance was doubtless enhanced by an order from Márquez that morning that anyone who communicated with the enemy in any fashion would be shot.

Agnes then requested written authorisation for her to negotiate in the name of the foreign officers and troops, but they thought this also too dangerous. They suggested that she proceed on her own and make two propositions to Díaz. The first was that he should permit her to go to Querétaro to advise the Emperor of the true state of affairs in Mexico City and to determine what he wanted to do. For this, she needed a seven-day armistice. If Díaz would not agree to this plan, she had a second.

She would offer him the surrender of all foreign troops, under the condition that he give his word of honour – in writing – that he would guarantee the life of the Emperor and the foreign troops should they be taken prisoner. Agnes did not believe in half measures.

But, how to get to Díaz? Magnus knew of a trusted intermediary. Agnes contacted her, and she agreed to arrange an introduction, for a fee, but meanwhile Agnes had to get back to Colonel León in Chapultepec, lest he become suspicious of her long absence. Once he was put into the picture, Agnes returned to the capital – riding a handsome black horse that the Colonel had loaned her. She described the trip.

> Meanwhile it had become dark, and when I, with my maid and Jimmy, approached the garita [gate], the sentinel called out, 'Who goes there?' In my surprise I made a very sad mistake, for instead of answering 'Amigo' I resolutely called out 'Enemigo!' The sentinel answered at once by a shot, but the bullet whizzed harmlessly past us. As I was, however, afraid of a more effective repetition of the dose, I sought shelter behind the arches of the aqueduct which runs there, and Margarita [the maid], frightened out of her wits, knelt down and prayed to all the saints of the almanac.

In the end she was able to identify herself and gain the city. When Díaz finally did receive her at his headquarters outside the capital, and heard the conditions under which the foreign troops in Mexico City would surrender, he refused to believe her. He was convinced that she wanted only to get to Querétaro with messages from the garrison in Mexico City to plan a new attack on the Liberals. Besides, he told her, he would not accept the surrender of the capital under any conditions, since he was sure to take it anyway. But if the foreign troops did surrender, he would grant them life and liberty. Agnes continued to plead to be allowed to go to Querétaro, and in the end he said he would give her a pass and a letter to General Escobedo.

Back she went to Magnus and the two Austrian colonels. They declined to accept Díaz's terms of surrender without checking first with the Emperor.

Then suddenly on 24 April she was informed that Díaz had ordered her out of Mexico. An adjutant handed her a passport, asked her to name the port she preferred, and said Díaz would provide an escort to take her there. It seems that Díaz was convinced she 'had tried to bribe his officers with money and fair words, which was a great crime; and that I was too dangerous a person to be permitted to remain in Mexico'.

Agnes wanted to see Díaz to straighten out the misunderstanding, but the adjutant insisted on her setting off at once. She balked. 'They might shoot me or put me in irons, but they should not compel me to leave the country.' They sent a carriage; she refused to get into it. She sat down at Díaz's headquarters and refused to stir for six hours. In the end, after elaborate negotiations, with intercessions by all sorts of people, Díaz agreed she could go to Querétaro – without an official escort.

She set off on 27 April with letters of recommendation to owners of haciendas, hotel keepers and other useful contacts, four good mules and 'a very bright yellow superannuated fiacre [cab]'. When she reached the height of Cuesta China, and could overlook the town, she saw at once its weaknesses.

> Little as I understand about military art, it seemed to me most injudicious to make a place like Queretaro as it were the keystone of the whole war. The town is surrounded by hills, which are most favourable to the establishment of batteries, and whence every street and every house can be seen. It is a regular mousetrap.

She went to the hacienda to whose owner, Carlos Rubio, she had been recommended, and from there made her way to Escobedo's headquarters across the little stream where Felix and General Moret had been forced back almost two weeks earlier. Escobedo received her in his simple quarters. He was to play a key role in the weeks ahead.

Mariano Escobedo (1827–1902) had supported Juárez from the outset of the War of the Reform, and fought vigorously against the French. When they triumphed, he took refuge in the US, returning to Mexico with a reorganised army in 1865 and joining in the offensive. Monterrey fell to him, and much of the northeast, and he defeated Miramón at San Jacinto, near Zacatecas, in February 1867, taking many prisoners, including French and Austrian soldiers and Miramón's brother. The prisoners were shot, but that was nothing unusual in those bitter days.

Agnes told him she had heard that Felix had been wounded, and she sought permission to go to him. He declined, adding that he did not believe her husband had been wounded, but he did offer to give her a letter to President Juárez in San Luis Potosí, who might help her. 'He said he knew my husband very well, and complimented me very much about him, observing that he was an extremely brave officer, as he had experienced to his great damage. He promised to treat him kindly if he should ever fall into his hands.'

Escobedo gave her an escort, and they set out in a carriage for San Luis Potosí at 3.00 a.m. It took three days to get there, a distance of some 125 miles. She was ushered into the President's office by his aide, José María Iglesias. She wrote of her first encounter with Maximilian's implacable foe,

> Juarez was a man a little under the middle size, with a very dark complexioned Indian face, which was not disfigured, but, on the contrary, made more interesting, by a very large scar across it. He had very black piercing eyes, and gave one the impression of being a man who reflects much, and deliberates long and carefully before acting. He wore high English collars and a black neck-tie, and was dressed in black broadcloth. The President gave me his hand, led me to the sofa, on which Jimmy had already established himself, and said he would listen to what I had to say.
>
> I told M. Juarez all that had happened in Mexico [City], and what I intended to do in order to bring the horrible bloodshed to an end, and requested him to permit me to go to Queretaro.
>
> The President said that he had not received any details from General Porfirio Diaz, but he supposed that I must have done something very dangerous as I had been ordered so suddenly to leave the country. He could not give me an answer until he had been better informed. If I would return with the escort to M. Rubio, and wait there for his answer, I was at liberty to do so, or to remain in San Luis.
>
> I told him that I would reflect on it, and give him an answer next morning. The President gave me his arm, and accompanied me through all the rooms to the head of the staircase, where he dismissed me with a low bow.

Her self-confidence, her nerve, her fearlessness were staggering. Remember, Agnes was still only in her middle twenties.

This was also Agnes's first meeting with Iglesias, whom she liked. He was a distinguished jurist, was Juárez's Minister of Justice, became President of the Supreme Court in 1873, and was briefly President of Mexico in 1876.

Failing permission to enter Querétaro, she decided to remain in San Luis, where she could keep abreast of the latest developments and be on the spot to act accordingly. Juárez also sent word that he wished her to stay.

She thus sat impatiently awaiting news until 10 May, when the city exploded with the clamour of church bells and the firing of cannon. She soon learned that Querétaro had fallen, having been 'sold to the Liberals for three thousand "ounces" by a certain Colonel Lopez'. The Emperor was a prisoner, she was told, and her husband wounded. She rushed to see Juárez to obtain his permission to go to Querétaro, but he was occupied and unable to see her. 'Under these circumstances I thought it best to travel without his permission.' This she did, and arrived without incident at Querétaro on 19 May, four days after the fall of the city.

9

The Prisoners

A Liberal officer had told Felix that Agnes was in San Luis Potosí, and he was in a frenzy to see her. She had gone to Escobedo at once after her arrival, and received his permission to visit the prisoners at the Teresita Convent. He gave her an escort, Colonel Villanueva, and she reached the convent on the morning of 20 May.

Felix, she wrote, 'was not shaved, wore a collar several days old, and looked altogether as if he had emerged from a dust-bin, though not worse than the rest of his comrades. To see him again under these circumstances affected me very much, and I wept and almost fainted when he held me in his arms.'

'Her news was by no means comforting,' noted Felix, 'for she said it was intended to shoot us all'.

Felix took her to the Emperor, still in bed with dysentery. This was the first time Agnes had met him. Ladies were not received at court in Chapultepec in the absence of the Empress, who had left for Europe before Agnes had arrived.

'I found him in a miserable bare room, in bed, looking very sick and pale. He received me with the utmost kindness, kissed my hand, and pressed it in his, and told me how glad he was that I had come.' Agnes sized up the situation and decided something had to be done to make the Emperor and the others more comfortable. She decided that Escobedo should see the Emperor, but first she went to get them some clean clothes. The

Liberal commander was quite willing to meet Maximilian, so she and Colonel Villanueva found a suitable carriage, and in the afternoon the party set off for Escobedo's quarters at the Hacienda de Hercules, a property belonging to Rubio.

They were escorted into the garden of the hacienda, Agnes on Maximilian's arm, where they found a company of Liberal officers and others, who greeted the Emperor with low bows.

> General Escobedo advanced, and offered his hand to the Emperor. We went then to the right, in a wide walk, where seats were placed for us. We commenced the conversation about indifferent objects; but this was rendered difficult by two bands, which made a horrible noise, drowning our voices. The Emperor told General Escobedo that he had instructed my husband to make some propositions in his name, and he and Colonel Villanueva retired to arrange that business.

In Felix's account of the meeting, he related that the Emperor spoke of abdication. He said he would surrender Mexico City and Veracruz, and requested again that his officers be allowed to go to the coast. Felix and Villanueva sat down to work out a document, the main points of which were that Maximilian would abdicate the crown of Mexico and undertake never again to interfere in its political affairs; that he would order his generals, Mexican and foreign, to lay down their arms and surrender their strongholds; that the foreign troops be allowed to march to Veracruz and embark for Europe; and that he too be escorted to Veracruz under guard with his household personnel and allowed to embark. This carefully negotiated instrument, duly signed by both parties, was never mentioned again.

The *New York Herald*, the *New York Times* and other newspapers had correspondents in Mexico, and both Salms mention particularly the kindness and helpfulness of the *Herald* correspondents. One of these reported on 21 May as follows:

> The wife of Prince Salm-Salm, an American lady – nee Agnes LeClerq – closely related to President Johnson,[9] made her way alone to San Luis Potosi to intercede with President Juarez for her husband's life as well as that of the Emperor. The lady had sped so far in her brave mission that yesterday, on her arrival here from San Luis, herself, the Emperor and Prince Salm-Salm had a long interview with General Escobedo, and I

have reason to believe that terms have been arranged by which the lives of most of the foreigners will be spared.[10]

This initial optimism was general in the foreign press.

The party, rather depressed, returned to the Teresita, where Agnes again busied herself with trying to make life more agreeable for the Emperor and her husband. Dr Basch commented in his memoirs that she was the only one trying to do anything to improve their conditions. She prevailed on Escobedo to move them to a comfortable and well-furnished mansion, but a number of his officers protested the favourable treatment the general was affording the prisoners, and they were moved instead to the Capuchin convent (22 May). The Emperor was forced to spend the first night in the crypt – to give him a foretaste of what was to come, the guard told him – but Escobedo moved him the next day. Blasio reported that all the rooms were 'damp, dark and gloomy', but at least in his new cell on the upper floor of the convent he had a view of the patio and orange trees.

On the twenty-fourth he was moved again, and Felix was instructed to tell him to prepare for solitary confinement. Word had come that he and the other prisoners were to be tried by court martial. They had waged war against the legally constituted government of Mexico, and would be punished accordingly. Maximilian was taken to a cell in the upper story of the convent. Miramón and Mejía, who were to be tried with him, were similarly treated. Colonel Palacios, a colleague of Villanueva who had been reasonably kind to the prisoners, let Felix know that there was little hope for the Emperor. He was, however, permitted to choose lawyers to defend himself. Principal among these were Mariano Riva Palacio and Rafael Martínez de la Torre, able Mexican lawyers, and Frederic Hall, an American who had met the Emperor in Mexico City and offered to come to Querétaro to help him.

The Emperor's cell measured some 20 feet by 13, with a camp bed, crucifix and a mahogany table holding two silver candlesticks. There was a second table and some chairs. The crucifix and silver candlesticks were a bad omen in Mexico: they were always placed in the cells of prisoners condemned to death.

When Agnes set out to visit Felix on the twenty-fifth she was extremely perturbed. She had learned for certain that Felix and the Emperor would be shot. There was nothing to do but for her to go again to Juárez in San Luis and petition for a delay in the trial. She explained her plans to Colonel Villanueva, and together they went to the Emperor.

They arrived at the Capuchin convent around midnight and roused Felix, and the three went to the Emperor's cell. He agreed she should go to San Luis. Villanueva advised him to write a letter to Juárez requesting two weeks to prepare his defence, and to consult with the lawyers from Mexico City. Villanueva helped the Emperor compose the letter. Agnes was instructed to give it to the President and to no one else.

Agnes had a considerable struggle securing a carriage and mules, and reached San Luis only after a hectic trip. The President received her, read the letter from Maximilian, and responded that he could not possibly agree to a delay. Agnes pleaded the Emperor's case with all the eloquence at her command, and then withdrew to await the President's decision.

> When I returned at five o'clock [Iglesias] came to meet me with a happy, smiling face, and without saying one word he handed me the precious order granting the desired delay. I was so overjoyed that I nearly hugged that worthy gentleman. I wished to see Mr Juarez in order that I might thank him, but he was out.

The cabinet meeting Juárez had called to discuss the issue was split, but in the end the moderates carried the day.

Agnes had a horrible trip back to Querétaro. It deluged rain, and at several places the road was so bad that she and her escort had to walk. Arriving in Querétaro, she went straight to the Emperor.

'I was worn with fatigue; my boots torn to pieces, and my feet sore; my hair in disorder, and my face and hands unwashed. I must indeed have looked like a scarecrow, but I was very happy and a little proud too.'

She found some American correspondents with the Emperor, one of whom left a written description of the encounter, which she quoted.

> A bustle was heard outside, the heavy door was opened, and a soldier announced 'La Senora!' In an instance Prince Salm-

Salm held the new-comer in his arms. She was the voluntary messenger, his wife, who had just arrived from San Luis Potosi from Juarez. Her face was sunburnt and soiled, her shoes were torn, her whole frame trembled with nerveless fatigue as she laid her hands upon her husband's shoulders. The Archduke came forward eagerly, waiting his turn. The Prince was heard to ask in a whisper, 'Have you had any success? What did Juarez say?'

Agnes told them the good news and the American witness described a highly emotional scene.

꧁ ❧ ꧂

In the meantime, Felix was concentrating on escape. Maximilian was against it at first, but Felix talked him around – the Emperor's military honour had been satisfied, he was only 35, and a lifetime lay ahead of him. Felix had become friendly with a European cavalry officer of the troops occupying the convent, and went to work on him. He told him: 'You are a lieutenant, and have not been paid for months. You see, most of the Mexicans, whether Liberals or Imperialists, are blackguards, and you have indeed very little chance here. I will propose something to you, by which you may make your fortune.' The officer accepted, and Felix accordingly informed the Emperor. But Maximilian rejected any escape plan that did not include Miramón and Mejía. Felix despaired at the Emperor's often unfortunate displays of nobility, but these were entirely consistent with his character.

Maximilian remained concerned with protocol and formalities, and on the twenty-eighth ordered Blasio to prepare letters of patent for Felix's commission as a general, retroactive to 14 May, when he had first broached the subject. He also made him an officer of the Order of Guadélupe (originally created by Emperor Agustín Iturbide) and Agnes a dame of honour in the Order of San Carlos, founded by Maximilian and Carlota.

The escape plot proceeded as might have been expected. Felix's European friend told him nothing could be done without bringing in the officer who commanded the guard near the Emperor's cell. So Felix had to tell him his plans as well. He

104

did admit to being nervous, but he thought the man to be 'an honest fellow'.

Felix arranged with a confidant in town to procure six horses, six revolvers and six sabres, all of which 'were to be concealed in houses by lady friends'. The cavalry officer was ready enough to attempt to save Felix and the Emperor, but he drew the line at Miramón and Mejía. Felix reported a rather comical scene in which the Emperor flatly refused to disguise himself by cutting off his beard, and made futile attempts to tie its two long points behind his neck.

The American lawyer Frederic Hall later identified Felix's confidant as 'an Italian rascal ... [who] received 2,000 dollars of the Emperor's money to buy six horses, saddles, equipment and pistols'. He bought materiel of inferior quality, not worth 800 dollars, and made off with the rest.[11]

It was at this point that Agnes returned from her second visit to San Luis. She was very dubious about Felix's plans for escape.

> Now I had not any confidence in the success of this plan from the commencement, though I assisted in it as much as I could. The plan was very excellent, but I put no trust in the men whom my husband employed. Two of them had deserted from the French army. They were inferior officers, who seemed not to have either the power or the pluck to carry out what they promised, but gave me the impression that they wanted only to extort money. I therefore had opposed the plan from the beginning, and insisted that the Emperor should address himself to a far higher authority.

The question that now occupied the minds of the little party was how best to make use of the stay granted by Juárez. They decided that Agnes should go to the capital and come back with Magnus and the two lawyers who were to defend the Emperor at his trial. She secured letters from Escobedo to Porfirio Díaz and from the Emperor to Magnus and others. The plan was suddenly derailed. Felix reported that Agnes could not find a conveyance to take her to Mexico City, but, knowing Agnes, this was unlikely. Agnes put the blame on Felix. The date fixed for the Emperor's escape was 2 June and, argued Felix, if it was successful there would be no need for Agnes to have gone, and if it failed and there was trouble, she would be needed in Querétaro. 'I had quite a fight with him about it in the presence of the Emperor,' she wrote, 'which, however, ended with my doing his will.' Nonetheless, a telegram was sent to Magnus asking him to come, bringing the lawyers. Maximilian called for Magnus because he assumed he could expect no support from the Austrian minister, Baron von Lago. Emperor Franz Joseph had made it abundantly clear to his brother from the beginning that he was in this alone, and not to expect aid from Austria.

The cavalry officer upon whom Felix was relying now complicated the plot further by insisting on including the captain who shared his room. Felix was thus obliged to bring a third party into the plot. Agnes was increasingly suspicious. Felix saw the Emperor at 2.00 a.m. on 2 June and all was set to go.

It was not to be. A telegram arrived announcing that Magnus and the lawyers were en route. The Emperor thus decided against flight that night. 'If a thunderbolt had fallen at my feet,' wrote Felix, 'I could not have been more aghast.' He implored the Emperor, but he responded, 'What would the ministers, whom I have invited here, say if they arrived and did not find me!' Felix commented that they would doubtless have been delighted to meet him anywhere else.

Both Felix and Agnes were exasperated. The Emperor seemed unable to appreciate the danger he was in and, said Agnes, was always rather leery of their escape plans. He now declared he would await the arrival of Magnus and the others; a few days more or less would not make any difference. The third and fourth of June passed nervously and idly as they all waited.

Felix, of course, had to put off the three officers who were now privy to the plan, and they were very unhappy, fearing discovery and the loss of the money they had been promised. They had been given some gold, but they wanted more. The infantry officer then told him that the plot might be suspected. He and his comrades had been flashing their gold around and suspicions had been aroused. They had indeed. On the fifth a Liberal general burst into Felix's cell and accused him of attempting to effect the Emperor's escape. If you repeat it, he barked, you will be shot.

He was marched to a more secure cell in the casino where all the field officers had been confined. Strict measures were imposed: the guards were trebled, no servants were allowed, nor wine, and knives and forks were taken away.

Magnus arrived on 3 June, followed the next day by Lago, the Belgian and Italian ministers and the French chargé, a M. Forest. The lawyers arrived on the fifth. When they learned that the trial was set to open on 7 June, they protested that they had no time to prepare a defence. Escobedo agreed to postpone it for 24 hours. The lawyers telegraphed Juárez and Minister of Justice Iglesias, and were granted another five days. The trial was now to begin on 13 June. Iglesias, Riva Palacio and Martínez de la Torre went to San Luis to plead for clemency, but Juárez was adamant: no further delay in the trial.

The two lawyers were loyal republicans, but at the same time well disposed toward Maximilian. They were also conscientious lawyers. They were shocked by Juárez's insistence on a court martial rather than a regular trial, and by the haste with which the preparations for the court martial were being pressed ahead. They were incensed at the threatened application of the law of 25 January 1862, which was central to the government's case. Juárez had issued the law in response to the landing of the European allies at Veracruz. It declared the allies to be outlaws, and mandated the death penalty for anyone who conspired with the international force to subvert the established institutions of the country.

Agnes had little good to say about the European ministers, with Lago taking the brunt of her scorn now and in future years when she had to deal with him. These gentlemen seemed to forget, she wrote, that they were not accredited to the Liberal government but to the Emperor, who was now on trial for treason.

> They further forgot that the Liberal Government cared but little for all those Powers whom they represented, as they knew extremely well that none of them could do them much harm, because they were protected by the United States, which protection proved powerful enough to drive out of Mexico one of the most powerful princes of Europe.

Agnes was convinced that, wrapped in their self-importance as representatives of the Great Powers, the ministers completely failed to realise that the Emperor might well be shot. They believed

Juárez would not dare have him executed and bring down the wrath of the European powers. To be fair, this was the common belief outside Mexico. Agnes thought otherwise; she had been listening to Mexicans who, however well disposed they were personally, were convinced that the Emperor would die.

The American attitude was equivocal. The US government had always supported a republican form of government in Mexico, its minister was accredited to Juárez, and indeed Doña Margherita, Juárez's devoted wife, had lived in New York since 1864. When she visited Washington in 1866 she was received with great respect and honours as the wife of the President of Mexico. On the other hand, though it had never recognised Maximilian, the government hoped he would be treated in a civilised fashion. The concerned European governments appealed to Washington to intercede on Maximilian's behalf, but Washington's ability to communicate with the Juárez government was hampered because its minister, Campbell, refused to budge from the safety of New Orleans. When finally on 11 June President Johnson sent him a stern order to get going, he pleaded illness and resigned.

The blow fell on 8 June. Word came from San Luis Potosí that the Emperor and all 12 generals would be court-martialled under the law of 2 January 1862, which meant death. All colonels received six years' imprisonment, lt colonels five, majors four, captains and foreign lieutenants two. Felix was included with the colonels, but he insisted on producing his general's patent, despite the commanding officer's attempt to dissuade him, and on being treated as the other generals. The subordinate officers were marched away on 9 June to be interned in various gaols around the country.

Rumour had it that the European ministers had brought large sums of money with them. Knowing the susceptibilities of his countrymen, Escobedo felt it prudent to isolate the Emperor, Miramón and Mejía from the other prisoners, and increased the guard. It became much more difficult to gain access to them.

'I was on a friendly footing with all the staff of Escobedo,' Agnes wrote,

> and I heard from them many things they would not have told others. My attachment to the Emperor, and my zeal in his cause, rather pleased them, and I am sure most of them secretly wished

me success at least, if they did not do so openly. From them I heard that the scene was now drawing to a close; that the ministers were utterly impotent, and that their interference would not do the least good. The only thing which could save the Emperor was escape. That was whispered in my ear by more than one.

Agnes found the Emperor more hopeful about his future. Magnus dismissed her fears as groundless. On 10 June the Salms once again discussed escape with the Emperor. Agnes pressed on him her plan of negotiating a plan, not with inferiors as Felix had tried to do, but with officers of rank, specifically Colonels Villanueva and Palacios, the latter of whom was the prison commander. She needed 100,000 'dollars' in gold from the Emperor, to be placed in Rubio's bank for withdrawals as needed. Magnus and the others kept assuring the Emperor that money was no object, but, she railed, they never seemed to be able to produce it.

A more sceptical note was struck by the French chargé, Forest. He visited the Emperor on 12 June and found him bedazzled by Agnes's escape plans. Forest thought the whole scheme both foolish and dangerous, and tried to convince the Emperor, but his words fell on deaf ears. He was particularly doubtful about Agnes's claim of influence over Palacios, and he argued to Lago that Agnes was an unwitting tool of traitors. But Lago was as mesmerised by her plan as the Emperor.[12]

The government having refused to grant any more delays, the trial opened on 13 June, in the Iturbide Theatre, before a board of seven officers. Generals Miramón and Mejía were present, but the Emperor claimed ill-health and did not attend. He was outraged at the prospect of being publicly humiliated by having to appear on a theatre stage before an audience of as many people as could cram into the stalls and boxes. 'This triumph they would not have,' wrote Dr Basch.[13] 'The Emperor made clear to me his firm resolution not to appear in the theatre.'

Agnes went to his cell with a note from Felix imploring him 'to lose no time by resigning himself to delusive hopes, but to prepare immediately for escape'. She told the Emperor that she had arranged for Villanueva to lead him outside the prison, where a guard of 100 men would be ready to escort him to the Sierra Gorda and so to the coast. 'The Emperor insisted on my following him close on horseback with Dr Basch. He was afraid of being betrayed and assassinated, and thought that the presence of a lady might be a kind of protection against such an atrocious act.'

In the usual way in which these plots seemed to corral increasing numbers of people, Villanueva advised Agnes that nothing could be done without Palacios, whose men guarded the Emperor's cell day and night. But to win over Palacios, Agnes needed money. The Emperor was, understandably, strapped for cash, but he said he would see what he could do to get hold of some 5000 dollars in gold.

Querétaro was a reasonably wealthy town, having been founded by the Spanish in 1531 to exploit its gold and silver mines. There were also prosperous merchants, several of whom – such as Rubio – had been very supportive of the imperial cause. The inhabitants of the town were also friendly. Nonetheless, it had just undergone a brutal siege, and one wonders where the Emperor hoped to find such a sum.

The Emperor had not, however, been able to secure the money by the time Agnes returned. He offered instead to give her two drafts, each for 100,000 dollars, signed by him and drawn on the imperial family in Vienna. He also held out hope of having the 5000 dollars for her by 9.00 p.m.

The affair of the two drafts involved the European ministers. Agnes never forgot the incident. The Emperor had wanted the ministers, especially the Austrian, Lago, to countersign the drafts, and Lago did so, in his presence. Some hours later, after Magnus had returned from another quick futile trip to San Luis, he declined to sign on the grounds that he needed instructions from his government. After all, he was being asked to participate in subverting an officer of the Mexican army. This line of argument caused Lago to change his mind. He panicked and cried out that they would all be hanged if they signed, and the other ministers agreed. Lago even seized a pair of scissors and cut his signature off the draft. Agnes remained contemptuous of his cowardice for many years.

Both Salms seemed devoid of any sense of realism. They were obsessed with escape – understandably – but their obsession seems to have blinded them. They scorned the European ministers for what they saw as timidity and stinginess, but might better have

been called prudence. How they expected their own wheelings
and dealings – the attempts at bribery, the scattering around of
gold, the constant visits to Maximilian – to escape notice is hard
to fathom. Escobedo was no fool; he doubtless had them under
constant surveillance, and they certainly would have had no
easy time cutting through the lines to get out of Querétaro. But
passivity was not their style, and they would not see what they did
not wish to see.

Agnes had already informed Villanueva – whom, Blasio noted,
accompanied her everywhere – of her latest plans, and she told
him that she planned to leave the prison at 8.00 p.m. and request
Palacios to escort her home. She would then detain him for a
chat and spring her plan.

She saw the Emperor again that afternoon. When she prepared to leave, just before eight, he gave her his signet ring.
'Then I left with a very heavy heart and filled with anxiety, for I
had before me a task of the highest importance, which I had to
accomplish with very insufficient means – two bits of paper, of
which the meaning was scarcely known to the person with whom
I had to deal.'

Palacios was an Indian with no particular education who had
distinguished himself in the army and won the confidence of
his superiors. He had a young wife, and an infant child whom
he adored. Agnes figured that since he was poor he might be
persuaded by a handsome gift of money to go along with her
proposal. The Colonel saw her home as planned, and she invited
him into the parlour. She spoke to him of the Emperor, and he
seemed to Agnes to be sympathetic. He probably was, especially
in the presence of this charming woman whose devotion to the
Emperor was so intense.

'After this introductory conversation, which lasted about
twenty minutes,' Agnes wrote,

> with a trembling heart I came to the point. It was a most
> thrilling moment, on which indeed hung the life of a noble
> and good man, who was my friend and Emperor. I said that I
> had to communicate to him something which was of the
> utmost importance to both of us; but, before doing so, I must
> ask him whether he would give me his word of honour as an
> officer and a gentleman, and swear by the head of his wife

THE PRINCE AND THE YANKEE

and child not to divulge to anyone what I was about to con-
fide in him, even if he rejected my proposition. He gave me
his word of honour, and most solemnly swore, as I desired, by
the life of his wife and child, whom he loved beyond anything
in this world.

Agnes then laid her cards on the table. She knew, she told Palacios,
that the Emperor would be condemned to be shot. He had to
escape. She had arranged the logistics with others, and all Palacios
had to do that night was 'to turn his back and close his eyes
for ten minutes'. His cooperation was vital to the success of the
scheme. She again harped on Palacios's humble circumstances and
how this windfall would secure a good future for him and his
wife and child. What would happen to Palacios if this requested
treachery were found out, she seems not to have considered.

She offered him the Emperor's draft for 100,000 dollars in
gold, to be paid by the imperial family of Austria, plus the 5000
she was expecting from the Emperor to distribute to his soldiers.

Palacios thought for a bit, and then said, with his hand on his
heart, that although he felt the greatest sympathy with Maximilian
and really believed it to be best for Mexico to let him escape, he
could not decide about such an important step in five minutes.
He also said he could not accept the draft. 'He took it, however,
into his hand, and looked at it with curiosity. The Indian could
not conceive the idea that in such a little rag of paper, with some
scrawls on it, should be contained a life of plenty for his wife and
child. A bag full of gold would have been more persuasive.' At
this point Villanueva stopped in, and then Basch, and the subject
was discussed no more. Palacios left about ten. The others soon
retired, to wait.

Palacios, of course, went straight to Escobedo and told him
everything. It is difficult to imagine how else Agnes thought it
would turn out. It never seems to have occurred to any of them
that Mexicans, even Indian Mexicans, also had a sense of honour.
There has also been speculation that the two Mexican colonels
set them up, but in any case the effort was a disaster.

Before Agnes was up in the morning, a guard was placed on
her door and every visitor arrested, including Basch. Escobedo
summoned her. Insisting that the air of Querétaro did not agree
with her and that she was looking poorly, he announced he had

a carriage ready to take her to San Luis Potosí. She thanked him, but said she felt quite well and preferred to stay. The general then exploded with anger, charging her with trying to bribe his officers and embarrassing him acutely after he had shown her so much kindness and treated her so well.

> 'I have done nothing, General, of which I need to be ashamed and what you yourself would not have done in my position.'
> 'We will not argue that point, Madame, but I wish you to leave Queretaro.'

Unable to sway him, Agnes was forced to prepare to leave, but she delayed as long as possible, and made life miserable for the unhappy captain who had been detailed to escort her. Escobedo refused, meanwhile, to allow her to see either her husband or the Emperor, although she was permitted to send Felix a few quick lines. She also reported, with some satisfaction no doubt, that Escobedo told Villanueva that he would rather confront a whole imperial battalion than an angry Princess Salm.

While all this was going on, Felix was pacing his cell in frustration and ignorance. He waited all of 14 June for news from Agnes. An Indian woman finally brought him Agnes's note that she had to set off immediately for San Luis Potosí. She was very sorry not to be able to see him, and could not at the moment give him an explanation. He sent her a sharp reply asking her to come, but she had already left.

He soon learned the whole story. He was suddenly transferred to a small chapel and locked in. His gaolers were furious that he had tried again to liberate the Emperor despite all their warnings.

❧❧❧

On the evening of the fourteenth, at the end of the second day of the trial, the court found the three defendants guilty, and sentenced to them to death by firing squad on 16 June.

In San Luis, Agnes went first to Iglesias and hence to the President. Juárez had been apprised of the escape plan, but he again received her courteously. She pleaded for the Emperor's life, but Juárez was implacable. The Emperor must die. Her husband, however, would not die, even if condemned to death, and he gave her, she wrote, his hand and his word of honour. In her efforts to get the execution delayed, she even wrote to President Johnson, 'whom I know well'. From Europe came a torrent of appeals from princes and politicians, even from Garibaldi and Victor Hugo. The fact was that the republicans in Mexico cared nothing for the opinion of European governments. European royalty held no mystique for them. Besides, Juárez must have taken a certain grim satisfaction in having in his hands a descendant of that Charles V whose soldiers had destroyed the Aztec empire and brought Indian culture in Mexico to ruin.

From Washington, Secretary of State Seward had no better luck. He had repeatedly urged Juárez to accord Maximilian and his party the humane treatment that civilised nations commonly show to prisoners of war, and he kept at it after the fall of Querétaro. He was under considerable pressure from European crowned heads, but he seems also to have felt sorry for Maximilian, and hoped that he would be allowed to return to Europe.

In Querétaro, Felix was in despair. He had learned that the court had condemned Maximilian and the two generals to be shot. He begged the Emperor to permit him to accompany him on his last walk, but Maximilian refused. 'He had made his peace with the world, and it would affect him too much to take leave of a person who was so dear to him.' Maximilian apparently feared also that Felix would do something rash, and the poor man probably had had enough drama by this time.

Then came word that the execution had been postponed to the nineteenth, along with the (erroneous) news that the Empress had died. The Emperor was very shaken. 'One string less that binds me to life,' he told Basch. Agnes had not been alone in her pleas for a pardon. Magnus and the two Mexican lawyers had also gone to San Luis to see Juárez and other officials. The foreigner did not get very far, but the Mexicans did get the President to agree to a three-day postponement. Fighting hard all the way, Riva Palacio and Martínez de la Torre had urged the President to pardon Maximilian – condemn him, but then show mercy – but Juárez refused to consider such a course of action. The execution was now set for 19 June.

The two Mexican lawyers had done their level best. Agnes was the more flamboyant pleader of Maximilian's cause, but the lawyers defended him on cogent and closely argued legal grounds. They were genuinely disturbed by the proceedings. Unfortunately, they were up against what for Juárez was a political necessity. For the sake of Mexican unity and the republic, the intruder in whose name so much blood had been spilled had to die.

Agnes now prepared for what was to be the greatest scene of her life. On the evening of 18 June she had another interview with the President.

> With trembling lips I pleaded for the life of the Emperor, or at least for a delay. The President said he could not grant it; he would not prolong his agony any longer; the Emperor must die tomorrow. When I heard these cruel words, I became frantic with grief. Trembling in every limb and sobbing, I fell down on my knees and pleaded with words which came from my heart, but which I cannot remember. The President tried to raise me, but I held his knees convulsively, and said I would not leave him before he had granted his life. I saw the President was much moved; he as well as Mr. Iglesias had tears in their eyes, but he answered me with a low sad voice: 'I am grieved, Madame, to see you thus on your knees before me, but if all the kings and queens of Europe were in your place, I could not spare that life. It is not I who takes it, it is the people and the law, and if I should not do its will, the people would take it and mine also.'

He again reassured her that Felix's life would be spared.

In the Palacio del Gobierno in San Luis Potosí, where Juárez lived in 1867, a wax-figure tableau in one of the rooms he occupied depicts the scene. Juárez stands by a table – the table on which he signed the order to execute Maximilian – his right hand on a book; at his feet kneels a richly dressed Agnes. The representation must give considerable satisfaction to indigenous Mexicans, who are understandably sensitive about foreign interventions in their country.

Back in Querétaro, news of the postponement of the Emperor's execution overjoyed Felix, always the optimist. 'I ordered a bottle of wine to drink good luck to the Emperor, and smoking my cigars and humming a tune, I paced my chapel, and even the horrid faces of the martyrs on the wall seemed to smile.' He still thought of escape. He described how he figured out that the wall of the little yard next to his chapel, which he could see from his window, was all that separated him from the street. If he could scale that wall, he would be free. All he needed was a rope. Would Agnes bring one, perhaps concealed in the mattress she had promised to bring? His celebratory mood was premature. On the morning of the eighteenth Villanueva told him the postponement was meaningless. The Emperor would die.

The Emperor and Basch drew up a list of persons to receive mementos. To Felix went his spyglass that he had used during the siege; to Agnes went the fan he had used in prison. The Salms had been a balm to Maximilian. Felix's loyalty was rock-solid, in contrast to that of his Mexican generals, who supported him in part because they had nowhere else to go. They had long ago forfeited any possibility of a pardon from the Liberal side. They fought loyally; they had no choice. Felix, on the contrary, had joined Maximilian of his own free will and stood staunchly by him. He was brave and, importantly, a German prince who gave Maximilian a link, however tenuous, to the Old World. Agnes, witty, charming and resourceful, had tried hard to keep his spirits up as well as doing everything she possibly could to save him.

They came for Maximilian at six in the morning of 19 June 1867. He went by carriage to the Cerro de las Campañas, accompanied only by a priest. Other than his valet and his cook, who followed in a second carriage, only Magnus attended the execution, and his account, written to the Prussian Chancellor, Count Otto von Bismarck, is the only one from an eye witness.[14] Magnus had sent a telegram to San Luis protesting one last time, but the Foreign Minister rebuffed him flatly. With Miramón and Mejía, the Emperor walked to the wall. Maximilian made a short speech in Spanish, in which he forgave everyone and prayed that he would be forgiven. The shots rang out and it was over.

A small chapel stands now on the Cerro de las Campañas, erected by the Austrian government in 1901 and paid for by the imperial family. It contains a rather pathetic little collection of Maximiliana. Looming over everything, on the very top of the hill, is an enormous, brutal statue of Juárez. There is no doubt who won.

Only Vidaurri and Márquez remained of the generals who were with the Emperor when he entered Querétaro. Márquez, after commanding the defence of Mexico City, went into hiding along with Vidaurri. When the city fell and Díaz marched in on 21 June, Vidaurri was discovered and shot. Márquez took three million dollars from the treasury and managed to escape, first to Veracruz and then to Havana. He was permitted to return to Mexico in 1895, but his unpopularity drove him out again. The Tiger of Tacubaya died in obscurity in Havana in 1913, aged 93.

The evening before his execution, Maximilian had given two letters to the bishop of Querétaro, addressed to his mother and to Carlota. They were seized by the authorities and the one to Carlota was opened. Written in French, it read,

> My beloved Carlota. If God permit that your health improve and you should read these few lines, you will learn the cruelty with which fate has stricken me since your departure for Europe. You took away with you not only my heart but my good fortune. Why did I not give heed to your voice? So many untoward events! Alas! So many sudden blows have shattered all my hopes, so that death is but a happy deliverance – not an agony – to me. I shall die gloriously, like a soldier, like a king vanquished, but not dishonored. If your sufferings are too great, and God should call you soon to join me, I shall bless his Divine hand that has weighed so heavily upon us. Adieu, Adieu! Your poor Max.[15]

10

Felix Rescued

Felix was by no means out of danger. As a general in Maximilian's army, he still stood under the threat of a likely death sentence. Agnes was stuck in San Luis, from where she wrote him a despairing letter. She had failed him and the Emperor. Juárez and his ministers had promised her that his life would be spared, she said, but Felix was not too confident. Sra Miramón had received the same assurances. In an interview by a lawyer on 23 June, he stoutly defended his loyalty to the Emperor. 'Did you know a lawful government existed?' he was asked. He was well aware of Juárez, he replied, but he recognised only the Emperor, and still did. He and Colonel Pitner, who shared a cell in captivity, were the only ones who wore their imperial uniforms after their capture.[16]

Ruminating on the whole sad affair some years later, and particularly on the role of the European ministers, he noted that Maximilian did not like Lago who, however, with a colleague, had been decorated in Vienna for their supposed role in trying to save the Emperor. 'I hope that this token of satisfaction from their living prince will compensate them for the poor opinion which the dead Emperor entertained for them.'

Only Escobedo could permit Agnes to return to Querétaro. He finally consented on 30 June, but cautioned her against any attempt to arrange an escape. Thus cautioned, she arrived on 3 July and gave her husband a charged revolver that she had concealed in her dress. She found him thin and pale, impatient and excitable. He thought only of escape, but in that she could not assist him. In his nervous state, she noted, he made life difficult for both of them, and she commented that he was 'not very amiable with the officers who guarded him'.

By 11 July, Felix's court martial seemed imminent. Anyone who counted for anything had left Querétaro, including Escobedo, so the couple decided that only from Mexico City could they hope for a reprieve. Agnes accordingly departed for the capital on the twelfth. The trial opened on 15 July, but Felix thought the whole thing a farce – he had, after all, been taken bearing arms against the government and that was punishable by death – and he refused to attend. He sent word that he was ill, and no one bothered with him. On the seventeenth the court announced that the generals would be shot on the nineteenth.

He prepared to die and talked with a priest. He asked for writing paper, wine and cigars, and wrote letters to his wife, his brother and other relations and friends. 'Then I went to bed, but did not sleep particularly well.'

Early on the nineteenth he was informed that his execution had been postponed five days, and on the twenty-second that it had been postponed indefinitely. Juárez had indeed promised Agnes that his life would be spared, but it also seems likely that the regime, now that it had finished off the Mexican principals, was simply not interested in foreigners like Felix. The execution of the Mexican generals settled old scores and, in a sense, had to be done. Felix was not particularly important as far as the Juaristas were concerned, now that they had won.

Life now became somewhat easier. The prisoners were moved back to the more comfortable quarters in the Capuchin convent, and Felix acquired an Indian servant named Eufemio, formerly in the household of the late General Mejía, 'who had no other thought but how he might help me escape'. Various impractical schemes were discussed and rejected. At least it kept his mind busy. The kindness of the citizens of Querétaro, who brought food and necessities, made up in part for the indifferent quality of the accommodations and the boredom. He wrote to Agnes in the capital to try for banishment, but she answered that there was no chance of that at the moment. The ministers with whom she spoke had lost interest, and felt they ought to be glad they were alive.

The generals learned of their sentences on 16 August: Felix got seven years.

Agnes returned to Querétaro on 8 September. She was allowed only one visit a day, and the guards were not always pleasant to her, but gradually conditions improved. Felix described the amusements and diversions thought up by the prisoners, including the French officers, who were a particularly lively bunch.

In late September they were allowed to go into the town on parole from 10.00a.m. to 2.00p.m. They usually breakfasted at Agnes's house and then went on to see friends. After a while Agnes received permission to visit Felix freely and stay till 10.00p.m. 'so that we could have a regular rubber of whist'.

The main worry of the prisoners now was the part of the country to which they would they be sent to serve their terms. The preference was for Veracruz, from where ships sailed for Europe. It was thus something of a blow for Felix to learn on 5 October that he was destined for Monterrey. Not only was that far in the north, but under the authority of Escobedo. He preferred Oaxaca under General Díaz. And so it happened. There was a sudden change of orders. On the ninth Felix and several other generals, including Castillo and the incompetent Moret – he of the failed attempt to break out back in April 1867 – marched out, headed for Oaxaca, Felix mounted, the others in three carriages. A crowd of well-wishers saw them off and plied them with all sorts of edibles for the journey. 'We halted,' wrote Felix, 'on the Cuesta China, the highest point near Queretaro. From there ... I turned a last sad look of adieu toward the Cerro de la Campana. The place we stopped was the same on which we had halted when we arrived with the Emperor.'

Agnes followed in a carriage. On the fifteenth Felix and his comrades arrived in Mexico City. They were lodged initially in a common prison, wrote Felix rather disparagingly, but were then moved to the convent of Santa Brigida, where a number of imperial officers were already confined. They marched through the streets of the city two by two, with Felix and old General Severo Castillo arm in arm at the head of the column. Felix writes of passing so many places of amusement he knew so well, and many familiar faces lined the route to cheer them on. The convent was a grand building, large and clean with a fine shady colonnade and many trees. The place swarmed with visitors all the time, bringing them fruit, flowers, cigars and other delicacies.

In a dispatch dated 18 October, the *New York Herald* correspondent reported on the transfer of Castillo and Felix to the convent, and went on to say, 'There is quite a feeling of sympathy for the Prince, especially among the American residents who were in the Northern army, many of whom knew him there. His friends in New York may be glad to know that he is in the best of health, and that he is as full of courage as ever.'[17]

Agnes and their friends now set to work getting Felix sent to Veracruz rather than to Oaxaca. Magnus visited him on 24 October with encouraging news. Prince Alfred, Felix's elder brother, had asked Count Bismarck to intercede, and he in turn had communicated with Gerolt, still Prussian minister in Washington. Gerolt raised the matter with Secretary of State Seward, who knew the Salms, and he instructed the US legation in Mexico to try to secure Felix's release.

In a cable to his Mexican counterpart, Seward said,

> The Prince ... was an ardent and efficient volunteer in our late war for the defense of the Union, whereby he entitled himself to the sympathy and friendship of this Government. For this reason, as well as that of comity toward the Prussian Government, I beg leave to commend the case of Prince Salm-Salm to humane and liberal consideration.[18]

Since June the US had been represented in Mexico City by Marcus Otterburg, who had been US consul there for some months and who had established good relations with Juárez, Díaz and others of the new regime. Otterburg had the field clear since the European ministers had all been accredited to Maximilian and were now thoroughly discredited. His intervention lightened the conditions under which Felix was held, and ultimately led to his release.

Felix, Castillo and other prisoners were now assigned to Veracruz instead of Oaxaca, and they and the others set out in the late afternoon of 25 October. They were marched not like generals and prisoners of war but rather like common criminals, two by two (with Felix and Castillo again in the lead) between a cavalry escort. Agnes wept to see them. She had been caught off guard, uncharacteristically, and only caught up with the party at the railway station, where a crowd of ladies had gathered to serve coffee.

The railway in those days stopped short of Puebla, so they resumed their journey on foot, reaching Tehuacan, headquarters of Díaz, on 31 October. They were hospitably received all along the way, and in Tehuacan Díaz was kind enough to invite them to dinner. Felix was allowed to roam around town at will. Those assigned to Veracruz left Tehuacan on 3 November, without an escort, Felix on horseback and armed with letters from Díaz to officials in Veracruz. The route of march took them to Orizaba and Córdoba to Paso del Macho, where the railway picked up again. In Córdoba Felix received a cable from Agnes that the Mexican Secretary of War had signed his release. She had argued, reported the *New York Herald*,[19] that he had been a colonel at the time of his capture, Maximilian having made him a general only afterwards. In fact, the Mexican government in early November proclaimed a general amnesty whereby all foreigners held since the end of the war were at liberty to leave the country. At 10.00 a.m. on the eighth Felix was back at the Hotel Diligencia in Veracruz, where he had suffered through a bout of malaria a scant year before, when the whole adventure had begun.

It was one thing for an amnesty to be proclaimed; it was another to get official notification to the authorities in Veracruz. While Felix was waiting for the order to arrive, he met some British naval officers in a coffee shop who offered to take him aboard their ship. As he was expecting the arrival of Agnes any moment, he declined. The next day the commanding general of Veracruz, who denied any knowledge of the amnesty, ordered Felix and Castillo confined in the island fortress of San Juan d'Ulloa, just offshore. The fortress, begun in the sixteenth century, was dilapidated and dank, the climate was hot and sultry, and Felix had an altogether miserable time. The Veracruz commander made life very unpleasant for these remnants of the imperial cause. Not surprisingly, Felix spent most of the time plotting to escape.

Magnus finally arrived with the release signed by Juárez himself, and Felix was set free on 13 November after a nasty few days. Still waiting for Agnes, he planned to take a ship leaving on 3 December, but the Veracruz commandant, who persisted in his hostility, insisted he take the very next ship leaving port. This was scheduled to sail on the fifteenth for France. Remonstrances were unavailing, so, leaving a letter for Agnes to follow, he went aboard. Magnus and Blasio were fellow passengers. He had just enough time to pay a quick visit to San Juan d'Ulloa and bid farewell to his old comrade Castillo (who was eventually freed thanks to Otterburg), and then set sail for Europe.

Agnes arrived the next day, and was understandably upset to have missed him. She decided to leave right away, and booked passage on a steamer to New Orleans, from where she made her way to New York. She had a fine time in New York seeing friends and being feted. She also went to Washington to see her sister Delia 'and also President Johnson, and other persons who had assisted my husband, to thank them'.

She sailed for Brest from New York on 28 December 1867 aboard the *Ville de Paris*.

Felix, meanwhile, had landed in St Nazaire after a crossing of 30 days, and after five days in quarantine headed for home. 'On the 24th of December, 1867, I was in the castle of my brother in Anholt, and spent a merry Christmas with my family, which I had not been able to do for many long years.'

❧❧❧

One can only stand in awe of Agnes. Mexico brought out all the talents she had honed during the Civil War. Then she had button-holed senators and governors and generals on behalf of her husband. Her drive for his promotion was relentless. In Mexico she soared to new heights. Here she was, still in her twenties, in the midst of an exceptionally cruel civil war, surrounded by treachery, dealing with a new set of generals and with the great revolutionary leader Benito Juárez himself.

She obviously was devoted to Maximilian and did all she could for his release. Only his two Mexican lawyers worked harder, but they argued the letter of the law as they read it, while Agnes was all passion. She walked when she could not ride, waded through mud, ducked as bullets sped by – in short, she was not afraid to get her hands dirty, which was probably another reason she was so contemptuous of the European ministers. She seems to have impressed everyone, on both sides of the conflict, with her bravery, though she must have driven some of them to distraction. Even Escobedo, writing 20 years later, referred to her dogged efforts to save Maximilian.

Wrote one British admirer,

> Her beauty, her grace, her wit, her zeal rendered her at once one of the most interesting and one of the most effective of the friends of the captive Archduke...Had Maximilian himself been endowed with only half her energy, or a quarter of her intelligence, he would never have found his way into Queretaro or, being there, he would certainly have found his way out.[20]

On the other hand, one wonders why Agnes, certainly a hard-headed and practical woman, became so enamoured of Maximilian, to whom she always referred in the most adulatory tones. Was the newly minted princess overcome by the idea of friendship with a Habsburg? Was she simply following her husband? More likely, her naturally kind heart went out to this unfortunate man who had suffered such bitter blows and stood alone. Agnes liked people, and she took instinctively to people in distress. The fallen emperor aroused her sympathies.

Then, too, Maximilian represented the kind of challenge that Agnes found irresistible. Tense negotiations with generals and Juárez himself was precisely what she was so good at. That she was doing all this in a foreign country and in a foreign language made the challenge even greater.

She did not, however, have much to say about the thousands of Mexicans who suffered and gave their lives to rid themselves of the rule of the French usurpers. She was not concerned with the principles of the imperialists or of the Juaristas; she was focused on Felix and Maximilian and their problems. She deplored the treatment meted out to the Indians by the Spanish conquerors, and she deplored the cruelties of the French to the Mexicans, but she did not take the argument any further. Mexicans do not play a significant role in her narrative.

As for Felix, he had sought war and action, and he found it. He fought bravely and well for the emperor he served – his family, after all, had been serving the Habsburgs for generations. Unlike his wife, this spoiled aristocrat had absolutely no sympathy for Mexicans, and he referred to them in generally derogatory tones. His diary is focused solely on the issues of war and the siege, and extrication from the doomed city; he never raises his sights higher. Contemporaries all agree on his bravery, but he remains a one-dimensional character.

Agnes, as usual, was convinced that without her Felix would fail. From the very beginning, five years earlier, she had watched him like a hawk – or mother – to be sure he did not stumble in some way. She was distraught when he marched off to Querétaro without her, and as soon as she could manage it she rushed to his side after the fall of the city. He was, in some ways, her creation, and she had to keep him safe and sound.

Whatever the case, all this was now behind her. The time had come for her to play her role as a Princess zu Salm-Salm on her husband's home turf.

PART III

Germany

11

Settling In

Agnes landed at Brest on 6 January 1868 after a rough crossing. She was tremendously happy to be reunited with Felix, whom she had not seen since he marched out of Mexico City on 25 October 1867, heading for Veracruz. They went to Paris, but he was anxious to take her to the Salm family seat at Schloss Anholt, and they stayed only a day or two – time enough for Agnes to do some shopping, of course. They doubtless strolled the avenues and enjoyed the cafes and restaurants. Perhaps, if the weather was clement, they crossed the Seine by the new Pont Solférino, opposite the Tuileries Garden, so Felix could show her the Palais de Salm. This had been built before the French Revolution by a prince of Salm-Kyrburg. Napoleon I made it the headquarters of the Legion d'Honneur (which it still is). But they did not linger in the French capital.

They did not attempt to see Napoleon or anyone else at the French court. The French government had abandoned their Maximilian to his fate, after all. Even if they had tried, it is doubtful that Napoleon would have seen them. He had had a highly emotional meeting with Carlota, and he certainly did not wish to tangle with yet another strong-willed woman from Mexico.

Agnes was a trifle nervous about her reception at Schloss Anholt. 'Though Felix had assured me that I should be received most kindly by his whole family, I still had some apprehensions, fearing the formal and ceremonious stiffness which I imagined to be inseparable from all Prussian families.' On arrival, she was glad to say, 'all my fears were speedily removed by the very kind manner in which I was received by my husband's brother and his numerous family'.

And numerous they were. Felix's eldest brother Alfred, aged 54, tenth Prince zu Salm and fifth Prince zu Salm-Salm, and his wife Augustine, a princess of the house of Croÿ-Dülmen, had ten children, five boys and five girls, aged from 31 to 15. In addition there was Wilhelmine, widow of Felix's older brother Emil, who had died in 1858, and her three children. Agnes liked 'Minna' very much, and they became good friends. They were the only two members of the family not born into princely families, which might have made for a special bond between them.

Schloss Anholt is one of several lake-girt castles in this stretch of German territory north of the Rhine, where the flat watery plains stretch across the Netherlands to the North Sea. It presents a grand sight rising from the lake that surrounds it. On the left stood – and still stands – the oldest segment, dating in part from the fourteenth century, firmly anchored by a great round tower, a remnant of the original twelfth-century fortification. On the right, connected by a small bridge, stood the stables and administrative buildings. The Salm family acquired the castle with extensive grounds and the lordship of Anholt in the mid-seventeenth century.

The family first came into view in the late tenth century and acquired the lordship of Salm in 1035. The scant ruins of the ancient castle are in the valley of the Salm River in the Belgian province of Luxembourg. A faction of the German nobility opposed to Emperor Henry IV elected Hermann I, Count of Salm, as German king in 1081, but he survived only three turbulent years. In the thirteenth century the family split into two main branches, Upper Salm and Lower Salm, and the founder of the former built another castle of Salm in Alsace, now also in ruins, near the town of Schirmeck. When the line of Upper Salm died out in the fifteenth century, its lands passed by marriage to a family that originated in the twelfth century and enjoyed the titles of Rhinegrave and Wildgrave, titles found nowhere else in Germany.

The members of the elder branch were created princes of the Holy Roman Empire in 1623, and shortly thereafter, in 1649, the incumbent Prince Salm inherited by marriage to its heiress the castle and lordship of Anholt. The Anholt lordship existed in the twelfth century and had been held by but two families prior to the Salms. The Salm line divided into Salm-Salm and Salm-Kyrburg at the beginning of the eighteenth century. The two lines were created princes of the Holy Roman Empire in 1738 and 1743 respectively, but Salm-Salm continued to enjoy the princely creation of 1623.

The history of the family was not particularly notable, but nevertheless it provided Germany with a long series of soldiers, bishops, a cardinal or two, and a noted botanist. Loyal Catholics, they served the Habsburg emperors faithfully, even though the tides of history eventually swept them under the suzerainty of the Protestant kings of Prussia.

Her brave words notwithstanding, Agnes must have felt somewhat apprehensive. For the first time, she was on Felix's home turf, faced with a whole new set of players whose dynamics were as yet unknown to her. She had dominated his life up to now; would she be able to continue to do so? From the dark panelled walls of the castle stared down on her row upon row of aristocratic ancestors. In the Great Hall, 60 feet long and floored with enormous planks that run its entire length, the portraits are particularly impressive (one of Felix hangs high up on the side of a window recess). There are splendid uniforms, frock coats and medals for the men; ribands, tiaras, jewelry and embonpoint for the ladies. Agnes had joined daunting company.

Perhaps somewhat defensively, she wrote,

> The house contains very fine halls, with an armoury and other relics of olden times, and above one hundred rooms. All this is very fine and noble, but it did not altogether correspond with the ideas I had about a princely palace. Used to the luxurious dwellings of the rich people in North America, everything appeared to me somewhat primitive.

The uncarpeted staircases and bare but highly polished and thus slippery floors bothered her – especially after she fell in her bedroom.

She settled down to a life of domestic amusements. She learned billiards and how to swim, there were rides in the country, on which she could demonstrate her equestrian skills, and a bit of hunting. After the Civil War and Querétaro, the peace and leisure must have come as a welcome relief. For a while.

⌁

Alfred and Felix were deeply concerned with the latter's future. Felix wanted to get back to the Prussian army again, but there were those debts from which he had run away. He was not able to rejoin the Prussian army while he was still a pursued debtor. When the creditors learned that the prodigal had returned, they swarmed round Alfred. He was willing to do what he could, but he did have a large family to maintain. He was also well aware, as Agnes put it, 'how shamelessly some of these usurers and sharpers had profited by the extravagance and carelessness of his younger brother'. Alfred was as eager as Felix to find a solution to these problems.

One can imagine that Alfred was perhaps a trifle impatient with his younger brother who had caused nothing but trouble – expensive trouble – before he went to America, and here he was back with an American wife of no background whatsoever. Beautiful and charming, yes, but no lineage. Felix had redeemed himself to some degree by his exploits in the American Civil War and in Mexico, and the stories he and Agnes told no doubt artfully enhanced his contributions to those conflicts. Nonetheless, here was Felix again, a potential source of trouble to this solid German *paterfamilias*.

It was finally decided that Felix should go to Vienna. Agnes went too, to call on the Archduchess Sophie, Maximilian's mother, as she had promised the late emperor. Agnes greatly enjoyed the trip up the Rhine, and was very pleased with Vienna, where they met old friends, including Dr Basch. Felix had an audience with Emperor Franz Joseph on 18 February. It was not a successful meeting. The Emperor, who was not a generous man by nature, had been deluged with requests for pensions and rewards from those who had served or claimed to have served his brother of Mexico, and he was sick of it. He had been against the whole idea from the very first, and now he was being hounded, which he clearly resented.

Agnes was furious that Lago, who had done so little for Maximilian, had managed to snare a decoration, whereas Felix, who had done so much, was not honoured. He was in the end offered a modest annuity, but turned it down as insultingly small.

Felix's presence in Vienna quickly became known, and his creditors managed to have him arrested. He had to pay a healthy sum of money – Alfred again – to get out. He decided it was best to leave Vienna for Munich.

On 27 February, Archduchess Sophie received Agnes. It was an emotional meeting. 'She was extremely kind, cried a good deal, and thanked me much for what I had done for her beloved son.' More importantly, she interceded with Franz Joseph to grant Agnes a respectable annuity, which was thankfully accepted. This was to be important for Agnes for the rest of her life. The Archduchess also sent Agnes a splendid brooch with a portrait of Maximilian. Sophie, a princess of Bavaria, had played a significant role in 1848, when Germany and Austria were swept by liberal outbreaks. She had persuaded the ailing Emperor Ferdinand I to abdicate, talked her own husband, the next in line, to waive his rights of succession, and brought forward her energetic 18-year-old son Franz Joseph to take over the imperial duties. Agnes must have sensed a kindred spirit.

From Munich the Salms moved on to Bonn, where they were well received by Counts Albrecht and Hermann zu Salm-Hoegstraten, of yet another branch of the Salm tree. The latter was always referred to as Uncle Hermann, and he seems to have taken a liking to the younger couple. But back in Anholt, discouragement set in. With no settlement of the debt problem in sight, the future looked dark. Alfred tried to reach an agreement with the creditors, but the more he was perceived as willing to help, the more importunate they became.

Alfred now suggested that Agnes and Felix leave Germany for a while, and they decided to join their old friends the Corvins in Switzerland. Corvin had held a post with the US Treasury Department, and then became a correspondent for the *New York Times*, returning to Germany in 1867. The Salms took a steamboat up the Rhine to Cologne and made an expedition to visit the ancient castle of the Salm Rhinegraves in Alsace. They continued to Basel, and from there travelled to

Constance on the lake of the same name, where they met the Corvins.

The two families took rooms in the Hotel Garni at Rorschach on the southern shore of the lake, near the town of St Gallen, with its ancient Benedictine monastery. Rorshach had been an important lake port in the Middle Ages, and preserved many old painted houses. Behind the town rose the Rorschacherberg, with views embracing all of Lake Constance and the mountains. The wooded hills were full of trails for pleasant walks.

Felix and Corvin went house-hunting, and found a reasonably comfortable castle for rent, Schloss Wiggen, with great views. Agnes loved the place, and the many titled neighbours. The Dowager Queen of Württemberg had a villa at Horn, just along the shore, and up behind town the Duke and Duchess of Parma had a place. The only drawback was the kitchen of Schloss Wiggen. 'It is true,' wrote Agnes, 'that the cooking apparatus of centuries ago was very insufficient, but we had all been used to camp life, and found it not very difficult to put up with little imperfections and simple fare.' The lake was lovely, the country charming. They found an unused bathhouse right on the lake at an uninhabited estate nearby, so they enjoyed bathing. The lake was famous for its salmon, trout and pike, so the two men spent a good bit of time fishing. The two couples took expeditions into the mountains, and made friends of all classes, from gardeners and fishermen up to those with grander titles. Felix worked on *My Diary in Mexico*, Agnes on her German. One senses that it was all a blessed relief from Anholt.

There were parties and picnics to neighbouring towns – Bregenz, Ragatz, Heiden, St Gallen – that 'interrupted now and then our monotonous but rather pleasant life, which would have satisfied me more if the unsettled state of Felix's affairs had not troubled my mind and embittered all enjoyment'. Felix went to Munich and Vienna to try to borrow funds, but without much success, and the scant news from Alfred was not very encouraging either.

In August they moved into a nice old house in Rorschach. Mrs Corvin went to Frankfurt, and her husband decided he preferred to live in town. But their amiable life continued. 'Our company was increased by Mr. Malpurgo, the brother of

Baroness Hauser, an agreeable young man suffering from the poetical fever.'

The social level began to rise. In September they were invited to visit Prince Karl Anton von Hohenzollern-Sigmaringen and his family, including his second son Karl, who in 1866 had been chosen by the Great Powers to become the ruling prince of Romania as Carol I. Their estate, Weinburg, was a short distance from Rorschach in the hills. Prince Karl Anton (1811–85) was the head of the elder branch of the Hohenzollern family that originated in the twelfth century and by the thirteenth had split into two branches. The elder Catholic line ruled a long slender territory stretching north from Lake Constance deep into the kingdom of Württemberg; the younger line moved from being burggraves of Nürnberg, to margraves and electors of Branden-burg, to dukes and kings of Prussia, and along the way became Protestants. In the sixteenth century the elder line divided into the branches of Sigmaringen and Hechingen, both of which were elevated to princes of the empire in 1623. Prince Karl Anton had a distinguished career as a soldier and diplomat, and from 1858 to 1862 was chancellor of Prussia (to be succeeded by Bismarck). As a result of the revolutionary upheavals of 1848–49, he and his cousin of Hechingen surrendered their previously sovereign principalities to the King of Prussia. When the Hechingen line died out in 1869, Prince Karl Anton assumed the title of Prince of Hohenzollern.

His sons achieved their own measure of fame. The second, King Carol I of Romania, ruled that country for 48 years and died in 1914. The eldest son, Leopold, was to play an important role in events ahead, as yet unshadowed.

Prince Karl Anton was very good to the Salms, and his wife, Princess Josephine, a princess of Baden, sent them flowers and fruit and visited them often in Rorschach. Agnes liked them both immensely. The Prince sympathised with Felix's predicament, and promised to help if he could. Only Jimmy was unhappy; he did not get along with the Hohenzollern hounds.

Tired of waiting for something to happen, the Salms finally decided to take matters into their own hands and go to Berlin to seek a suitable posting for Felix in the Prussian army. They arrived in the Prussian capital on 7 October, and after a short hotel stay took lodgings in the Kanonierstrasse. The Corvins were there, and Magnus – his brother was an important banker – as well as Felix's young nephew Maximilian, who was a lieutenant in a regiment. There was another round of visits, expeditions and theatre parties, and although Agnes claimed she did not feel up to it, Felix insisted. *My Diary in Mexico* was published, and was well received.

Felix was received by King Wilhelm I in early November, and was invited to dine. It is a mark of Salm social status that this younger son, with all his problems, should be so treated by his monarch. News of Felix's exploits in the US and especially in Mexico had preceded him, and the King was curious. Agnes noted that he returned from the dinner 'much elated and full of good hopes'. Among the many old friends and comrades who gathered around was Prince Kraft von Hohenlohe-Ingelfingen (1827–92), a contemporary of Felix and, more importantly, a major general of artillery who stood in favour with the King. He had performed brilliantly during the Seven Weeks' War with Austria in 1866. Agnes reported that he was a frequent and helpful visitor.

Having honed her skills on the upper ranks of the aristocracy, Agnes was ready for royalty. On 14 November she was received by Princess Maria, the wife of Prince Karl, younger brother of Kings Friedrich Wilhelm IV (d. 1861) and Wilhelm I. She was a princess of Saxe-Weimar and sister to Queen Augusta. This was Agnes's introduction to the royal family. The Salms were then presented to Prince Karl, a field marshal and an artillery officer. He was also a firm reactionary, viscerally opposed to any breath of liberalism. These visits broke the ice, and many court personages came to call, undoubtedly consumed with curiosity about this young American and her husband, whose exploits in the New World were by now well known. Agnes mentions a list of notables, including Bismarck, the Prussian chancellor, and the elderly George Bancroft, historian and since 1867 American minister to Prussia.

Countess Seydewik, principal lady-in-waiting to Princess Maria, took a liking to Agnes and introduced her around. At one gathering (as with many, I imagine) talk turned to Mexico. Agnes had a sharp exchange with one gentleman, with whose views she disagreed. She was not at all discomfited to learn that he was the Austrian minister.

At long last, Magnus brought the news that Felix had been appointed major in the 4th Grenadier Guards, 'Queen Augusta' Regiment. Somehow the debt problems seem to have been finessed. Agnes observed that had Felix not left Prussian service as a lieutenant, he might now have been a colonel, but Felix was overjoyed, and insisted he preferred to be a major in the Prussian army than a general in the American and Mexican armies. Corvin noted that many in the officer corps still resented that Felix had left Prussian service for Austrian all those years ago, and blocked his appointment as colonel.

Agnes now reached the top. She and Felix were granted an audience with Queen Augusta. 'I could not get rid of the idea,' she wrote,

> that she would receive me sitting on a throne under a dais, surrounded by superbly-arrayed ladies watching every movement of mine with a criticising eye.
>
> I was ushered into a room, where I did not see anything I had anticipated, and looked in vain for a throne. In that room was a fine and stately lady, elegantly but simply dressed, whom I took for one of the Court ladies who would lead me to the presence of the Queen. I stopped irresolutely, but when Felix made his lowest bow and kissed the extended hand of that lady, I became aware that I was standing before the Queen herself. Though somewhat disappointed and perplexed on account of the absent throne and royal state, I was more than indemnified in looking on that noble, beautiful face, with its inimitably gracious and benevolent smile.

The conversation turned to Maximilian and his fate, and the Queen spoke highly of Agnes's role in the tragedy. Agnes went on,

> Though she did not say that she expected to see me with an Indian feather dress and a bow and arrows, or at least a revolver in my belt, I imagine that the Queen was somewhat disappointed in her turn at seeing a woman such as those of whom she saw daily many prettier and more remarkable.

(Agnes's syntax occasionally shows German influence.) The audience lasted about half an hour, and the Salms then withdrew. This was the beginning of Agnes's unstinting admiration for the royal couple, an admiration that was positively cloying at times.

King Wilhelm I (1797–1888) was a military man through and through. He had been in the army from his twentieth year, had held increasingly important commands, and in 1854 was created field marshal. He was no dilettante; he had made a serious study of German and other military systems, and was exceedingly well informed. In politics he was very conservative, but he was an eminently practical man of shrewd common sense. He saw the necessity of bending to the prevailing liberal winds, and supported the constitutional movement. But he believed first of all in order and discipline, and thus it was that he commanded the army that put down the revolutionary movement that convulsed the grand duchy of Baden in 1848–49. He was appointed military governor of the Rhineland and Westphalia in 1849, with Coblenz as his headquarters. When his brother King Friedrich Wilhelm IV was incapacitated with mental illness in 1858, Wilhelm became regent, and on the King's death in 1861 he succeeded to the throne.

Concerned about the threat posed by the ambitions of Napoleon III, the regent launched a reform and strengthening of the army. In 1862 the now King appointed as chancellor the arch-conservative Bismarck, an avowed enemy of liberalism but a man known and trusted by Wilhelm to advance the cause of Prussia. For Wilhelm believed deeply in the destiny of Prussia as the leader of a united Germany.

Cut from a rather different cloth was Augusta (1811–90). She was the daughter of the Grand Duke of Saxe-Weimar, and was raised in the liberal atmosphere of that court. Her grandfather had issued the first constitution of the many German states. Goethe was a frequent visitor at court, and gave Augusta a poem on her ninth birthday. She was known for her keen mind and good judgment, and she was interested in liberal theories. She exercised a moderating influence on her husband – she and Wilhelm were married in 1829 – and as a result she was detested by Bismarck, who attributed any and all setbacks to his plans to her supposed machinations. She was sympathetic to Catholic causes, another source of conflict with Bismarck, especially when he launched the anti-Catholic *Kulturkampf* in 1871. Augusta had a keen interest in hospitals and nursing care and she often visited Florence Nightingale on trips to England.

In their personal lives, the royal couple were kind and considerate. They were unfailingly kind to both Agnes and Felix.

12

Back in Service

Felix went off to join his regiment in Coblenz on 21 December 1868. Agnes followed him three days later, and they celebrated their joint birthday (28 December) in Bonn.

Agnes was soon swept up in wholehearted and rather uncritical admiration of all things Prussian. She enthused about the Prussian army and its splendid training, skills and dedication. Rival states will not come up to scratch, she suggested, if they 'do not endeavor to create among their people the same spirit and feeling which pervade the Prussian nation'. The military caste played a leading role in society because of its training, and she lauded the superior military skills of the generals and the superior tactics of their troops. Discipline was the key. And the Prussian officers were 'gentlemen in every respect'. She was rapidly falling into line.

The most egregious example of her admiration comes in the introduction to her book, written after the establishment of the German Empire in 1871. 'The old German Empire has risen like the phoenix from its ashes, in richer glory than ever before, and from its radiant throne a fresh and wholesome current is sweeping over our globe.' This from a young American woman of heretofore pronouncedly democratic views is rather startling.

On the other hand, Agnes had never, till now, lived an ordinary settled life in an orderly society. As a child, her family life was apparently non-existent, certainly unsatisfactory. The circus and the stint in Havana provided her no reliable framework. The Civil War years in the US and the frantic year in Mexico gave little chance for rest and reflection. Now she was living in a very ordered and orderly society, married to a man with a good military appointment and a lofty aristocratic lineage that gave her access to the highest persons in the land. She can perhaps be excused for her rather uncritical enthusiasm for the powers that were. They were comforting to lean on.

The 'family' of the Queen Augusta Regiment in Coblenz took her in with great cordiality, to which she responded with gratitude. 'After the unsettled life I had led since my marriage,' she wrote, 'and all the exciting scenes I had witnessed, I longed for rest and a home. My hope of finding in little Coblenz a happy home was increased by this amiable behavior of the ladies toward me.' She took to them immediately. They were good solid German *Hausfrauen* who ran sensible homes and led sensible lives. There was, however, as always, a sprinkling of old maids 'with eyes as searching as those of custom-house officers, tongues as sharp as razors, and wagging even in their sleep'.

The military society did have rules, however, that required a newcomer to measure up. The officers of the regiment were proud of their traditions, and their wives were equally proud, and the regiment expected them all to follow the social codes. One had always to be mindful of the interests of the corps. Agnes did not find all this confining. On the contrary, it was very comforting to belong.

They found a house in Coblenz, and Agnes went back to Berlin to buy furnishings. She stayed with the Corvins. Queen Augusta received her again on 13 February 1869, and the King came in for a few minutes. He praised the pages of her diary that had been appended to Felix's book, and complimented her on her *tapferes Benehmen*, her 'valiant behaviour'. 'I now understand perfectly the love and enthusiasm with which my husband always spoke of his Majesty.'

One of Felix's cousins showed up, Prince Karl zu Salm-Horstmar (1830–1909), a religious enthusiast who had loaded Felix down with tracts and pious books when he went to the US in 1861 to bring enlightenment to the savages. Agnes had discovered the bundle still unopened when they were living in New York

City, and had presented the tracts to their Methodist landlord, 'acquiring by this gift an undeserved odour of sanctity'. Prince Karl had ceded his rights of succession to the principality to his younger brother, who duly succeeded their father. His wife, a Hohenlohe princess of ancient lineage whom he married late in life, did not share her husband's views and she was particularly annoyed by his renunciation of his ancestral rights. She tried hard to find a legal flaw in the cession, but to no avail.

The Salms moved into their new home in Coblenz in early April. They had ten rooms on the first floor of a good house.

Agnes was very happy in the first home of her own she had ever had, surrounded by furnishings of her own. Life was very agreeable. There were lots of parties and much gaiety, along with trips into the country by horse and river steamer. 'To atone in some way at least for our, not idle, but rather gay and useless manner of living,' a number of the Catholic ladies formed a sewing circle that made clothes for the poor, mended priests' vestments and otherwise occupied themselves with charitable works. The Queen visited frequently. Coblenz was one of her favourite residences, and she had done much to beautify the town while her husband had been governor of the province in the 1850s. Among her projects was a fine promenade running a mile and a half or so along the Rhine.

Coblenz was a lovely town of, in 1870, some 27,000 inhabitants. It sits at the confluence of the Mosel and Rhine Rivers, which gives it a double river frontage. Prussia gained possession in 1815, and turned it into one of the strongest fortresses on the Rhine, with a permanent garrison of some 5000 men. The royal palace, where Queen Augusta retained apartments for her spring and autumn visits, stood – and still stands – in a fine park along the Rhine. It was built before the French Revolution by the last Prince-Archbishop of Trier, Clement Wenceslaus of Saxony, who lived there until the French expelled him in 1794. On the north side of the palace gardens was the Clemensplatz, where military parades were held daily and there were concerts on Wednesdays. Dominating the town from the cliffs across the Rhine was the powerful fortress of Ehrenbreitstein, a stronghold of the archbishops of Trier from the early middle ages, now considerably strengthened by the Prussians.

The country round about is very mountainous, with a particularly rugged region stretching eastward from the opposite side of the Rhine. Castles dot the hilltops, and the steep banks of the rivers are draped with vineyards. Along the Mosel they are almost impossibly vertical. Just below Coblenz the Lahn River flows in from the east, cutting its way through the schist plateau. The valley sides are steep, but they fall back here and there, leaving narrow fertile strips. Good red wine comes from its vineyards. The area has many hot springs of real or imagined medicinal value, and there have been spas there since Roman times.

The most famous of these is Bad Ems, which grew up on the right bank between the river and the rocky cliffs, but gradually spread to the other side. There were fine mansions, many hotels (Der Englischer Hof, Der Russischer Hof, l'Hotel de Flandres, the Prince de Galles, etc), bathing establishments and the famous Kursaal or Casino, the focus of aristocratic life. The height of the season was from mid-July to the end of August. Between six and eight in the evening, one could find the most brilliant society promenading in the gardens of the Kursaal. But those seeking the benefits of the healing waters were up early. These were taken between 7.00 and 8.30 a.m. The countryside offered a plethora of walks, some of them quite strenuous, taking one up the wooded and vine-clad cliffs to the splendid views on top. A railway connected the spa with Coblenz, so one could get easily back and forth. Agnes was soon to know the scene well. It was a favourite of the King.

Though Agnes liked the swirling social life, she was perfectly happy to stay at home working with her new sewing machine or taking long walks with her friends, or listening to music on the Queen's new promenade. She quickly took to the amiable German habit of sitting in public gardens 'amongst smoking and beer-drinking people of all classes'. Felix was busy with his regiment, and she had time to fill.

Everyone looked forward to the Queen's visits to Coblenz. All agreed that she was a kind and gracious woman. She gave two great balls each year, to which everyone was invited, and also two informal-dress *cafés-dansants* in the palace gardens, where there was dancing on the gravel. The Queen also gave more select parties and dinners where dress was formal.

Agnes went often to Bad Ems when the season opened. On 10 July she went to call on the Grand Duchess Alexandrine of Mecklenburg-Schwerin, the King's sister. The Grand Duchess was particularly fond of dogs, so Jimmy was expressly invited as well. King Wilhelm sent for her on 20 July to join him at Bad Ems, and they walked together for half an hour. Agnes saw the King several times, and remarked on his 'noble open face'. One ran into everybody on the promenade at Ems, so it was not surprising that Agnes met their old friend Gerolt, still Prussian minister in Washington.

She also met George Bancroft, the American minister in Berlin, for whom she did not care in the least. Bancroft (1800–91) was a distinguished American historian and political figure who, in his capacity as Secretary of the Navy in the 1840s, founded the US Naval Academy at Annapolis, Maryland. He was US minister in London (1846–49) and in Berlin (1867–74). He was very pro-German. Agnes complained that he courted and flattered the Germans but neglected Americans, who were quite put out with him and pressured President Grant to recall him. At a dinner one evening, he remarked that in the event of a war between France and Prussia, the US would certainly side with Germany. The French were infuriated, and a diplomatic furore resulted. Bancroft also fell out with Gerolt, and by spreading malicious rumours succeeded in getting him recalled from Washington in 1871 after 25 years of service.

Social life at the top in the summer and autumn of 1869 was hectic. A few examples will set the tone.

In August, at a ball at Ems, she met Felix's first cousin Eleanor, wife of the Duke of Osuna, whom she married when the duke was Spanish ambassador to St Petersburg. Mariano Tellez-Girón y Beaufort was one of the grandest of Spanish grandees, holding eight ducal titles, one *conde-duque*, four marquisates and a string of lesser titles. Agnes and the Osunas hit it off very well, even though the duke was given, said Agnes, to 'rather doubtful jokes'.

On 11 August the Salms dined at the castle of the Princess von Sayn-Wittgenstein along with the King and Queen, Prince Reuss, the Prussian minister to St Petersburg and others.

After a couple of weeks at Schloss Anholt unwinding and shooting partridge, they plunged into the November whirl at

Coblenz. Agnes made no mention of problems with creditors. With Felix now an officer in the Prussian army, perhaps some arrangements had been worked out, either by him or by Prince Alfred.

They went to Neuwied, a few miles down the Rhine, to pay their respects to Princess Elizabeth of Wied on the eve of her marriage (16 November 1869) to Prince Carol of Romania. Elizabeth (1843–1916) was a protégée of Queen Augusta, who had invited her to Berlin to pursue her studies. Elizabeth wrote poetry and highly romantic novels and dramas under the pseudonym of 'Carmen Sylva'. More practically, she did a great deal in Romania to organise orphanages, schools for the blind, soup kitchens for the poor and other such endeavours. With her charitable interests, she and Agnes must have had much to discuss. On the tenth, at a party given by the Queen, Agnes was presented to Louise, Grand Duchess of Baden, a daughter of the Prussian monarchs. Grand Duke Friedrich's cousin was married to their old friend from Swiss days, Prince Karl Anton von Hohenzollern-Sigmaringen. It was all very family, and Agnes was happily in the middle of it.

On the seventeenth the Queen gave an extended-family breakfast: the Prince and Princess of Hohenzollern, the Prince and Princess of Wied, parents of Elizabeth, the Prince and Princess of Romania, the Count and Countess of Flanders, Princess Solms-Braunfels etc. They dined at Neuwied, where Agnes had a long talk with Philippe, Count of Flanders, son of Leopold I of Belgium and thus brother of the unfortunate Carlota of Mexico. His wife Marie was a daughter of Prince Karl Anton.

On 28 December 1869, the Salms celebrated their birthdays at Schloss Anholt and that of Prince Alfred on the twenty-sixth. Despite the glitter and the glamour, however, all was not well. Wrote Agnes,

> It is true Salm's wishes had been gratified; he was in a position in the army of which he was proud; we had a little home; society treated us as well as could be; and their Majesties and the whole Royal Family received us in a manner which affected me very much and raised the envy of many. In other respects we were not to be envied, however, for our position and our means to maintain the same were out of all proportion.

She was becoming increasingly bitter about the discrepancies in circumstances between them and other members of the family. The high titles and social advantages that Felix and Agnes enjoyed did not translate into the financial support they needed to live, or, more to the point, to live in the style the ever-improvident Felix thought was his right. She was infuriated by ancient laws that allowed two brothers to be treated so differently. Here was Alfred in his magnificent castle, enjoying the substantial rents from the broad acres he owned, while Felix had to exist on a major's pay and some small family annuities. Alfred had indeed been generous – that she admitted – but it was galling to be obliged to depend on his good will.

Her feelings of injustice were increased when she compared the merits of her husband with those of other members of his family. 'A long time ago,' she wrote, 'their ancestors had been men of fame; but since two centuries there was scarcely one amongst them who had done anything worth the notice of the world, whilst my husband at least had won fame for himself'. He was a prince, too, and deserved more equal treatment.

She faced up squarely to Felix's extravagance. They might have been able to stay within their income, she wrote, had Felix lived like other majors, but he

> was a Prince, and even if he had wished to economise, for which, however, he had little talent, in consequence of his education, he could not live so quietly and retiredly as prudence would have advised, for propriety required of him more than from other officers of his grade. Though I saw all the evil consequences of such a course, I had to submit, and being obliged to fulfill the social duties expected from a Princess, and being also by no means free from the inclinations of other women, I did as I was told was proper – and tried not to think of the end. In this I succeeded tolerably well up to the end of the year, but knowing that its first days would bring an immense number of little bills, I greeted the first of January with a very heavy heart.

She had known of Felix's extravagant ways for years, of course, especially after the whole story of his debts gradually came out, but this was the first time his profligacy had an important impact on their ability to lead a comfortable life. Agnes must have retained some sense of good New England thrift and was probably outraged at his carelessness. They must have argued about the situation, but she was helpless to do anything. Princes were supposed to live like princes, and that was that in their circles. She was also quite aware of how much she was enjoying their social standing, and that probably irritated her in her heart of hearts as well.

Back in Coblenz in January 1870 the bills arrived 'in shoals', as she had predicted, but she had to go on with their lives in the usual way. 'The season was not over yet, and teas, suppers and balls had to be attended.'

Most of January they spent in Berlin. They had a long audience with Crown Prince Friedrich and his wife Victoria, daughter of Queen Victoria. Agnes attended a reception at Court attired in a yellow silk gown with a six-foot train worn hanging over her left arm. And at last she had her wish to see the King and Queen sitting on their thrones raised about the level of the floor. It was at a concert, and the Salms were seated in the third row. The next night they went to a ball at the Royal Opera House and then they returned to Coblenz for another round of gaiety.

> How I longed for the end of all these balls, and thank Heaven, it came soon, for the one I gave on 28 February was the last of the season. We had eighty-six guests and the ball went off to the satisfaction of everybody. I danced every set, with young and old, and made myself as amiable as I could.

She did not feel well, however, and when the dancing was done she went to Berlin to consult Professor Dr Wilhelm Busch who had been recommended by Prince Alfred. Busch (1826–81) was a renowned physician, and had been head of surgery at the Johannis Hospital in Bonn for ten years. His textbook on surgery, published in two volumes in 1860, quickly became essential reading for aspirants. He was also noted for his research into the treatment of cancer. This proved to be an extremely important contact for Agnes, who was much taken with the doctor. He was a kindly family man who treated Agnes almost as a daughter, despite the similarity in their ages.

When the Queen urged the ladies of the Queen Augusta Regiment to learn how to nurse the sick in military hospitals,

Agnes leapt at the chance and went to see Busch and his staff. She was eager to learn how to dress wounds and to assist in operations. Busch was pleased with her earnestness and competence, and agreed that she should go through a course of surgery at a later date.

A promotion now came through for Felix, and in mid-April he took command of the Fusilier Battalion. Agnes surmised that this was partly due to his reputation as commander of the Cazadores in Querétaro, an experience in which the King had expressed great interest.

Spring came, and with it a new social round. Agnes reported on all this in great detail, but she confessed to feelings of foreboding that she could not shake, and that affected her health. The Queen arrived, and Coblenz and Bad Ems were again a whirl of activity.

On the promenade one afternoon she ran into the Osunas, Felix's cousin Eleanor and her ducal husband. They were sitting on a bench and chatting when up strolled Tsar Alexander II of Russia. He knew Osuna well from his days as Spanish ambassador in St Petersburg. He sat down on the bench, and the Salms were presented to him. After half an hour of pleasantries, the Tsar strolled off, unattended save for a large mastif.

This was not as extraordinary as it might sound. Alexander was a German prince who happened to sit on the Russian throne. The Romanovs had been marrying German princesses for generations. The last ruler of pure Russian blood was Empress Elizabeth, who died in 1762. Alexander's mother and grandmother were German princesses, and his great-grandmother was Catherine the Great, a princess of Anhalt-Zerbst. He was King Wilhelm's nephew, his mother being the King's sister. He was married to a princess of Hesse, a grand duchy across the Rhine from Coblenz. He had aunts and uncles, brothers and sisters married to Germans. He came frequently to Germany and was often in Bad Ems in the summer.

Most importantly, the Tsar had an only daughter, Maria, who usually came with him. Her marriage prospects were the buzz of Ems and other watering spots where gathered the aristocratic German ladies who were as much at home in genealogy as in their Bibles. In the end, Maria married in 1874 Prince Alfred, Duke of Edinburgh, the second son of Queen Victoria.

In late May Agnes began her studies at the hospital in Bonn. She assisted at several of Dr Busch's operations and learned how to dress wounds. Of the operating room, she wrote that she 'admired the consummate skill of the Professor, who cuts off a leg or an arm in an incredibly short time'. She was not feeling well, however, and her doctor recommended that she spend some time at Ems taking the waters. She repaired thereto in mid-June.

She saw a good deal of the King, who one evening invited Agnes and the Duchess of Osuna to join him at the theatre. He sat between them, and they had a jolly evening. Prince Albrecht, youngest brother of the King, now joined their circle. But her spirit remained troubled, and her health not as robust as she would have liked.

> Though I was not insensible to the kindness shown to me by everybody and the distinction bestowed on me by the most exalted personages, which would have made many others perfectly happy, I was as sad as could be when alone, a feeling of dread always hanging over me like a thundercloud. This feeling was made worse by reflecting on my position, of which the outside contrasted too strikingly with the real state, and which perhaps was not guessed at by others. I was treated as an equal by persons to whom thousands of thalers were as insignificant as were to me so many groschens, and Heaven knows what trouble I had to keep up appearances, when even the expenses for my gloves were more than I could afford. However, I was in for it, and could not retreat, though I shuddered at thinking of the end. I tried to forget it, and to pursue my course with as good a mien as possible.

Back in Bonn, she went to Busch's house for a consultation.

> Seeing Mrs. Busch surrounded by such pretty, healthy children, a blessed mother and wife, happy in every respect, and comparing her condition with mine, I felt quite wretched, and had a crying fit which made me quite angry, for I was afraid she would tell the Professor, who always treated me like a child, and would have laughed at me.

Once again the question of the Salms' childlessness arises. Why? Agnes obviously wanted a child: witness this outburst and the strange case of the fleeting 'adoption' of her infant nephew in

Dalton, Georgia in 1866. Felix came from a perfectly healthy family. His oldest brother had ten children; his deceased older brother had three. With a house of their own at long last, this would have been a logical time to start a family. Agnes was perhaps a bit lonely amidst all the superficial glitter of their lives, and a child would have given her life a focus and a purpose now lacking. Did she discuss the matter with Felix? Did he still not want to be bothered? We do not know. One can speculate endlessly, but there was to be no child.

13

The Franco–
Prussian War

European politics that summer of 1870 were taking an ominous turn. Bismarck had been working for a decade or more to make Prussia the dominant power in Germany and in Europe, supplanting France. In 1866 he had manoeuvred Austria into war and decisively defeated her in a matter of weeks.

The peace treaty brought Prussia much new territory in northern Germany, and Bismarck coerced Prussia's neighbours north of the river Main into forming the North German Confederation, dominated of course by Prussia. The next step was to bring the south German states, chiefly Bavaria, Württemberg and Baden, into the confederation, but this would take some doing. It was clear to Bismarck that the creation of a powerful German state would seriously alarm the French, already nervous about the increase in Prussian strength, and he came to regard war as inevitable if he was to fulfil his master plan. He had been running rings around Napoleon III for years, usually managing to keep France neutral or at least ineffective. Now the time had come to act. But he needed an excuse.

Providence put one in his way. Queen Isabella II of Spain had been deposed in 1868, and the provisional government of Spain sought a new monarch. At length an offer was made to Prince Leopold von Hohenzollern-Sigmaringen, the eldest son of the Salms' friend Prince Karl Anton. Bismarck saw quickly that placing a member of the Prussian royal house, however distant the relationship, on the Spanish throne would outrage France. Bismarck recommended that King Wilhelm approve the candidacy, but the King was totally averse. In the absence of the King's consent, Leopold declined the offer. Bismarck was not so easily deterred, however, and went to work behind the scenes. On 19 June, Leopold announced that he would accept the offer after all, and the King reluctantly gave his approval.

Amazingly enough, all this had been kept secret, but on 2 July the Spanish parliament inadvertently let the story out. The French were livid. Napoleon III could not let this pass. His authority had been weakened by a string of diplomatic reversals, including the very costly Mexican fiasco, and his popular support was ebbing. To accede to the enthronement of a Hohenzollern in Spain would mean the end of his reign. The French government, reflecting the sentiments of Napoleon and Eugenie and of the rabidly anti-Prussian duc de Gramont, the foreign minister, issued a strong statement that put Europe on notice that war was imminent. In addition, Gramont sent Count Benedetti, French ambassador in Berlin, to Ems to take up the matter with King Wilhelm and to ask him to order Leopold to withdraw. The King refused, saying it was none of his business, but he did send an emissary to Leopold to urge his withdrawal (11 July).

The next day, Karl Anton withdrew his son's candidacy. This was a triumph for the French government and an unexpected blow to Bismarck. The affair might have ended there had not the French government made a fatal miscalculation. War fever was high, and the French were convinced of their military superiority. Gramont ordered Benedetti to return to Ems and demand that the King not only acknowledge publicly that he approved the Prince's resignation but also promise never to allow Leopold to renew his candidacy. The King could only reject such a demand and cut short the discussion. Bismarck now had his chance to provoke war.

But to return to Agnes. The crisis was the talk of Ems, of course, but in the meantime the social whirl continued. Felix and the Queen Augusta Regiment arrived and passed in review before the King. That evening in Coblenz the Queen gave a dinner and dance at the palace for some 200 people. The King was not in attendance, but rather at Ems, where he preferred to pass his leisure time. It had become the custom for Agnes and her friends to wait on him there, and this evening the Queen urged them to leave the party and go to him. Thus it was that she witnessed the confrontation between Benedetti and the King on the promenade.

As the King left Agnes and her friends and walked away, Count Benedetti stopped him and said something, at which

> our noble sovereign became two inches taller, and his kind face acquired an expression that I had never before seen upon it. Making an impatient movement with his hand...he went away alone, leaving the oily Frenchman quite petrified. All who were near were very curious, and the news of this rather strange occurrence ran like wildfire through all Ems, creating great excitement.

The King did refuse the outrageous French demands, but he informed Benedetti that he had received confirmation from Prince Karl Anton that his son's candidacy was indeed withdrawn. Benedetti persisted, however, at which point the King terminated the discussion, politely but firmly. The simple facts of the interview were reported to Bismarck by telegram on 12 July. This was the famous 'Ems telegram' that Bismarck altered in such a way that it gave the impression that the French minister had insulted the King and that the King had snubbed him. Bismarck claimed he had not changed one word, which was true, but he had eliminated a crucial, conciliatory paragraph.

He saw that the doctored telegram was widely publicised on 13 July, which had the desired effect of whipping up national sentiment on both sides. France, confident of its superiority, declared war on 15 July. In point of fact, both sides were aching for war, the French to humiliate Prussia, the Prussians to settle once and for all which state was dominant in Europe.

Agnes had not wasted a moment. When war became imminent, she wrote the Queen asking permission to go with the army as a nurse. The King left to return to Berlin and a sombre mood descended on society. Ems cleared out as people hastened to return to their homes and prepare for the war.

Felix came for her, and brought her back with him to Coblenz. The city was filled with soldiers and reservists joining their regiments. They poured in by the thousand from all directions. Not all could be properly quartered, so many bivouacked in the streets or found shelter in barns and sheds.

The Queen took leave of her regiment on 17 July and returned to Berlin. She told Felix that she had received Agnes's letter, was very pleased at her offer, and that she might join the army at the proper time. Agnes went the next day to Bonn to look at hospitals and start her training. Busch agreed to take her in the field should he go, and she and several other ladies plunged into hospital work. Busch was now appointed Surgeon-General to the VIII 'Rhenish' Corps. Agnes was very pleased, 'for now I was sure of having the best opportunity of nursing my husband in case of his being wounded'.

Back in Coblenz, on 22 July the Corvins arrived to stay with them. Corvin was headed for the front as correspondent for several newspapers. Mrs Corvin was intent on hospital service. Corvin remarked of his old friend, 'The prince was all fire and flame,' ready to distinguish himself, though he feared he might be killed this time. Agnes's sister-in-law Minna arrived from Schloss Anholt with her eldest son Florentine, who was joining Felix's regiment as a lieutenant. Felix told Corvin, 'I felt some pangs of conscience at having persuaded my sister-in-law to let her boy go with me. That ambitious little fellow will certainly always remain by my side, and I should be extremely sorry if he were killed.'[1]

The Salm household was in an uproar of preparation, as indeed was every household in town. The Queen Augusta Regiment assembled in full strength, and the next day, 26 July, the whole army moved out towards the French border. Corvin had attended a review of Felix's regiment and wrote,

> When the regiment charged with the bayonet and with cheers, the men seemed to see the enemy already before them, for their faces were glowing with excitement. Prince Salm, I am sure, felt more proud to command his thousand men than he ever felt when commanding his American brigade.[2]

Agnes wrote,

> I had wished so much to go with the regiment, to be near my husband, for I always imagined that nothing could happen if I was with him. Count Waldersee [the regimental commander] was willing, and said if I really wished to go I might go in the

hospital waggon, but Salm was decidedly against it and I had to submit.

Then, too, wives did not accompany the Prussian army on the move.

She put on a brave front, but underneath she was filled with dread and premonitions of disaster. She realised that thousands of other wives felt the same way, but that was no consolation.

> When clasping my brave Felix for the last time in my arms, it was like a leave-taking on a death bed; and when he was gone, and even the sound of the horses had died away, it seemed to both of us, Minna and myself, that we had heard the rattling of the funeral car. Silently we fell into each other's arms in a close embrace, mingling our tears; and our fervent prayers for husband and son went up together to the throne of the Almighty.

But, she decided, work was the best therapy, and she quickly got down to business. Busch gave her a letter to Prince Pless, head of the sanitary commission formed jointly by the Knights of St John and the Knights of Malta.

These two orders were descended from the Order of the Knights of the Hospital of St John of Jerusalem, founded in the twelfth century in the wake of the first crusade to look after the health and well-being of pilgrims to the Holy Land. Driven thence by the Muslims, the order settled in Malta in 1530, where the knights remained until Napoleon seized their island realm in 1797. The nineteenth century saw the gradual recovery of the order from this low point, and its reconstitution with a greater emphasis on providing hospitallers than military knights. It remained, however, an order open only to titled aristocrats of impeccable lineage. As befitting the head of one of Germany's oldest houses, Prince Alfred was a knight. The order's Grand Bailiwick of Brandenburg had become Protestant at the time of the Reformation, and had suffered diminution along with the parent order, but it was revived in 1852 by King Friedrich Wilhelm IV as the Order of St John. In times of national emergency, the Johanniter joined with their Catholic brethren to provide hospital and medical services on the battlefield.

Agnes went next to Anholt to see the family. She tried to persuade Alfred to give her a horse, but he had none to spare what with three sons – his heir Leopold, and his brothers Karl and Alfred – already in the army needing mounts, and two more – Florentine and Maximilian – eagerly waiting their turn.

She had to get back to Bonn, but no trains were running on a regular schedule, and they were jammed with troops. In Cologne she managed to link up with Prince Leopold, ex-candidate for the Spanish throne, and one of the Saxe-Weimar dukes who had a train assigned to them, and on that she reached Bonn. On 30 July, Prince Pless sent her back to Cologne to get authorisation for her planned nursing career. She returned to Bonn wearing her new white armband with a red cross and riding in the rear car of the train with the conductor.

Finding a horse turned out to be a major task. Agnes did not intend to be a simple nurse. That was easy. She set her sights much higher. She wrote,

> I wanted to be in a position to do more and to be officially attached to the staff of the army like an officer. Everybody to whom I spoke shrugged his shoulders and declared such a thing to be impossible. It is, however, my belief that the only way to success is not to believe in impossibilities, and further it is one of my practical rules if I wish a thing always to ask it directly from the highest authority.

This was the old Agnes speaking; her juices were flowing again.

The authority in this case was the commander of the 1st Army, General Karl Friedrich von Steinmetz (1796–1877). He had a fearsome reputation, but that only spurred Agnes on. She managed to secure an interview, and explained what she wanted: namely, to be permitted to accompany the staff on horseback and to be allowed forage and quarters for her horse and herself. The general met this extraordinary request with silence. He then sent for the quartermaster general, and Agnes got what she wanted – except the horse. There were none to be had. She finally managed to buy what she referred to as a 'double pony' from a hotel proprietor for 200 thaler, but it had never been saddled.

Miss Louise Runkel now appears in the story. Agnes had decided that she needed a competent assistant and companion to help her in the work ahead. She asked around, and Princess Elizabeth of Wied recommended Miss Runkel. The two younger women had studied together in Berlin under the aegis of Queen Augusta. Miss Runkel was an accomplished nurse who knew how to treat the wounded. She was a hard-working, no-nonsense type, and she and Agnes hit it off at once. Miss Runkel was particularly eager to go with Agnes because she had two brothers in the VIII Rhenish Corps in which Busch was surgeon-general. Agnes gladly took her on.

Agnes, Miss Runkel and the pony left Coblenz by rail for Bingen, upriver near Mainz, and from there made their way across country to Trier where Steinmetz had his headquarters. At one point the pony gave Agnes fits, and tried to unseat her by jumping into a ditch and rolling over. Agnes said she performed some acrobatics that astounded the onlookers, and finally brought the beast under control.

Felix's nephew Leopold joined the ladies in Trier, and on 4 August they left by train for Saarlouis, a frontier fortress town south of Trier. They caught up with Steinmetz at Tholey, north of Saarbrücken, where they were billeted in a large brewery. Admiral Prince Adalbert of Prussia, a cousin of the King, turned up and invited them for dinner. His kitchen had not yet caught up with him, but Agnes rose to the occasion. 'As a dinner without anything to eat is still worse than Hamlet without Hamlet, I suggested to the Prince a picnic dinner, priding myself on my two ducklings [that she had acquired in Saarlouis] which the notary's wife in Tholey had roasted for me the day before.' Alas, they were not ducklings. 'They proved to be the patriarchs of the tribe and to judge from their toughness they must have been the very duck couple which Noah took into his ark.' They managed a supper of sorts, she said, to the sound of guns booming at Spicheren, just south of Saarbrücken.

Prussia had long prepared for this war, and was able to swing its troops into position – by rail – within a few days. From right to left, or north to south, on the Rhine stood the 1st Army under Steinmetz, the 2nd Army under Prince Friedrich Karl, nephew of the King, and the 3rd Army under Crown Prince Friedrich of Prussia. King Wilhelm had overall command of the German forces (for Prussia had been joined by Saxony, Bavaria, Baden, Württemberg and other German states), with Count Helmuth von Moltke as chief of staff. The French were not nearly as well organised, and their generals were subject to continual political pressures from Paris. They did, however, have two advantages, the fast-firing Chassepot rifle and the *mitrailleuse*, an early machine gun. Both had been developed after Prussia defeated Austria in 1866, and began to look like a real menace.

Paris was frantic for action, and a French army drove forward to the Saar River and occupied Saarbrücken on 3 August. Three days later they were obliged to withdraw from the city to the adjacent heights of Spicheren. News had come that the German 3rd Army had thrown the French back from the frontier fortress of Wissembourg to the southeast on 4 August. Steinmetz reoccupied Saarbrücken on the sixth and opened a terrific artillery exchange with the French on Spicheren. The noise of artillery brought German reinforcements to the scene, and a fierce battle with many casualties ended with the French pulling back to the west, abandoning their toehold in Germany. The German 3rd Army, pushing deeper into France, defeated the French again at Wörth and moved on a broad front to the line of the Moselle River, where they halted on 17 August to await developments.

Agnes and Miss Runkel went to Saarbrücken as soon as it was safe to do so. Her arrival was noted by none other than Corvin, who was at the front in his capacity as newspaper correspondent. He saw 'a whole host of army surgeons arrive with the Princess Salm on horseback'. They fell into each other's arms. She was surrounded, he wrote, by knights of St John. Corvin had little use for them, a bunch of rich noblemen who thought more of themselves and their own comfort than of the wounded, despite the huge amounts of provisions placed at their disposal. Some of the Johanniter were intelligent, practical and self-sacrificing, he allowed, but at least three quarters of them might better have stayed home and out of the way.[3]

The two women visited all the major hospitals, but Agnes remarked that the whole town was a hospital, with the wounded lying in every yard and house. The surgeons did their best, but the machinery of the sanitation commissions was not yet in full flow, and there was much disorder. Food was very scarce, despite the efforts of the townspeople, and Agnes had to set out to see what she could find. She reported some success from private citizens, but the pickings were slim. She also managed to get some food to a pen of French prisoners who had not eaten for two days.

These difficulties were grist for Agnes's mill. She remembered that in Cologne she had met Baron Edward Oppenheim of the wealthy banking family, who was also a member of the central committee of the Sanitary Commission. When he learned that Agnes was to be attached to the surgeon-general of the VIII Corps, he invited her to turn to him if she ever needed provisions for the wounded. She therefore telegraphed him to send 250 mattresses. They arrived in short order, along with many other useful items.

> August 8 was a busy day, for from the morning until ten o'clock at night I was dressing wounds, and comforting and nursing the dying. I am not very sentimental, but the sights I saw and the scenes I witnessed would have pressed tears out of a stone. Habit, however, soon blunted the edge of this feeling suffi-ciently not to interfere with my duty. Had this not been the case, I could not have endured it for three days.

The next day saw more of the same. Her brother-in-law Alfred, who took his hospitaller duties seriously, arrived and managed to find lodgings in a comfortable private house for them. She and Busch rode over to Spicheren to check on the wounded French-men. They found 180, destitute of everything. They returned to Saarbrücken over the bloody battlefield of 6 August, where the dead were still being buried. She commandeered an empty wagon she found in the street and drove to the depot of the Knights of St John, where she loaded up with provisions. Miss Runkel drove the wagon to Spicheren to distribute the supplies to the French prisoners while Agnes visited hospitals.

King Wilhelm, who was commander-in-chief of the allied German army, crossed the frontier on 11 August with Bismarck and Moltke.

'On August 11,' she wrote,

> I was all the morning with the professor in the hospitals assisting him in some wonderful operations. As many of the wounded in the citizens' casino required good and strong beef soup and other strengthening food, and Dr Busch said 'they must have such things or die,' I went to the kitchen of the

King and coaxed the head cook, who at once promised to attend to my wishes. After a time I went over with a soldier carrying some very large pails, which the brave chief of the royal kitchen batteries filled with delicious broth, fortified by good beef merged in it. As nobody was at hand to carry it, and the royal headquarters were not far across the street from the casino, I carried two of the pails myself.

Just when I was crossing the street, a carriage swept round the corner with His Majesty the King in it. Though not ashamed of my work, I felt rather embarrassed at being caught thus, and put the pails down behind me, screening them with my dress, when the King, who had seen me, stopped the carriage and descended. He came towards me, grasped my hand, and said very kind words which I shall never forget. Smilingly looking around me to discover the cause of my embarrassment, he saw my two pails, and when I told him that I had stolen them from his kitchen for his dying brave soldiers, the expression of his face became still kinder, and he said to me that I had done quite right, and that I was at liberty to rob his kitchen to my heart's content.

Corvin confirmed her story and was much amused by the incident.

And so the days passed, with Agnes rounding up supplies for the sick and wounded, making them as comfortable as she could and attending Busch in operations. There was an outbreak of dysentery that carried off a number of soldiers, and Agnes herself came down with a bad cold.

She was constantly nagged by fear of what might be happening to Felix, and finally determined to get closer to the front. She knew he was near Metz, but transportation was almost impossible to find, and she was told it would take at least eight days to get to Nancy, south of Metz. On 18 August she was filled with the most terrible forebodings amidst vague news that there was fierce fighting near Metz. On the twentieth she and Busch were in Saarlouis, where trains were arriving with the wounded from the front. She spotted a soldier from Felix's battalion but he could not – or would not – tell her anything.

The French had by now fallen back on the fortress city of Metz on the Moselle River. The Prussian high command ordered the 1st and 2nd Armies to advance westward south of Metz and across the Moselle. The Germans got it into their heads, all evidence to the contrary, that the French were in retreat across the river towards Verdun, and they seemed always to be surprised when they encountered an army instead of a rearguard. It proved to be a costly failure of intelligence. Moltke, a careful military planner, expected the French to be where his reading of military strategy indicated they should be. He overlooked the fact that the French staff was not always able to make purely military decisions, but had to bow to often ill-judged political decisions made in Paris.

Napoleon had indeed determined on a retreat, and on 8 August he put Marshal Achille Bazaine in command of the Army of the Rhine. We last saw Bazaine decamping from Mexico; his reputation survived the Mexican disaster, and in 1870 he was called again to command. The retreat commenced, but the next day Napoleon received urgent messages from Paris demanding that he stand fast. The Empress Eugenie and the war party would hear nothing of retreat. The German army thus encountered south of Metz not the rearguard but a formidable French force. After a fierce battle with heavy losses on both sides, the French fell back on the Metz forts. The Germans were now across the Moselle, and stood to the south and west of Metz.

The King and Moltke arrived on 17 August, and decided to draw up the 2nd Army on a north–south line to be ready for any eventuality. There was still uncertainty as to the exact strength and position of the French. Thus on the eighteenth the German order of battle was, from north to south, the XII 'Saxon' Corps under Crown Prince Albrecht of Saxony, the Guards under Prince August of Württemberg, and the IX, VIII and VII Corps under the Prussian commanders Manstein, Goeben and Zastrow. Felix's battalion was in the Guards.

Prince Friedrich Karl, commander of the 2nd Army, suddenly discovered that the five corps of the French Army of the Rhine stood on his right flank, and a rapid change of plan was necessary. The whole German army thus pivoted to the right and faced east, where the French forces were drawn up on a long ridge running north from the vicinity of Gravelotte, with their centre at Amanvillers. Due again to faulty intelligence, the Germans thought Amanvillers was the northern end of the French line. Not until a German force attacked did the high command realise that the French were dug in as far north as the village of St Privat-la-Montagne.

A quick march north brought the Guards to the village of Ste Marie-aux-Chênes, below and to the west of St Privat. Emerging from the protection of the village and a stretch of woods, they faced a broad open field that rises very gently toward St Privat for perhaps a mile. Just before the village, the gradient suddenly grows steeper. The defenders thus had an absolutely open line of fire. They were armed with the new Chassepot and *mitrailleuse*. The great advantage of the Chassepot was that it was faster loading than the Prussian rifle and had a range of 1500 yards as opposed to the 600 yards of the Prussian needlegun. The battlefield of St Privat was tailor-made for them.

At 4.30 p.m. on 18 August 1870 the Guards were drawn up in an arc from Habonville to Ste Marie, a distance of some 2 miles. The 4th Brigade of the 2nd Guard Division, consisting of the 'Emperor Franz' and 'Queen Augusta' Regiments, stood roughly in the middle. They were the first to move out, laden down with packs and equipment. 'Advancing at the double with drums, flags and mounted officers to the front, the brigade's initial advance was most impressive,' wrote one historian of the battle.

> Having covered the first half of its course, at approximately 1,500 yards the Chassepots of [the defending] infantry, untouched at this stage by any supporting fire from the German guns, opened fire. It has been estimated that an average French division armed with Chassepots could deliver approximately 40,000 rounds per minute. Within a matter of minutes, both regiments were literally shot to pieces, losing most of their officers, the 4th Guards all their officers. Two gun batteries moving up to give the brigade close fire support for the expected final assault were cut down before they could unlimber.

By 5.20 the survivors were pinned down still some 800 yards from the village.[4]

From another historian's account of the massacre:

The field officers on their horses were the first casualties. The men on foot struggled forward against the chassepot fire as if into a hailstorm, shoulders hunched, heads down, directed only by the shouts of their leaders and the discordant noise of their regimental bugles and drums. All formation disintegrated: the men broke up their columns into a thick and ragged skirmishing line and inched their way forward up the bare glacis of the fields until they were within some six hundred yards of St. Privat. There they stopped. No more urging could get the survivors forward...If anything was needed to vindicate the French faith in the chassepot, it was the aristocratic corpses which so thickly strewed the fields between St. Privat and Ste. Marie-aux-Chênes.[5]

Among them was that of Major Felix Prince Salm-Salm. More than 8000 of his comrades fell with him, killed or wounded, mostly in the first 20 minutes of the fray. In total at Gravelotte–St Privat, the Germans lost more than 20,000 killed and wounded, against 13,000 French casualties, plus 15,000 prisoners.

The archives at Schloss Anholt contain an excerpt from the *History of the Queen Augusta Guard-Grenadier Regiment* written by a fellow officer.

Colonel Count von Waldsee [the regimental commander], who set everyone a shining example through his personal bearing and who kept his horse always in the midst of his Grenadiers, was now severely wounded by a shot in his stomach. He insisted, nonetheless, that no one should drop out of the firing line on his account, he refused every offer of help and took himself off with the utmost exertion to the nearest field hospital. Likewise the next ranking officer in the regiment sank down, struck in the leg. The next in seniority, Major Prince Salm-Salm...took an enemy shot that smashed his right arm. He stanched the flow of blood with a handkerchief, gripped with his left hand his saber that had fallen to the ground and led his Fusiliers forward. Another shot struck the already-wounded arm and finally, as he stormed ahead paying no attention to his wounds, he was knocked to the ground by a third shot in his chest. To the chaplain who stood near his bed [in the field hospital] he asked with breaking voice: 'Are we victorious?' On receiving an affirmative answer, he said: 'Then all is well. Console my wife. Commend her to the Queen and assure her likewise of my full devotion.' So died Prince Felix Salm-Salm, a German hero.

He had been carried back to a field hospital in great pain from his wounds. The divisional chaplain and his servant, Köster, attended him, but they could do little save ease the pain. He died that night. Soldiering had been his profession and his delight, and he died as he would have wished, in the service of his king.

The Saxon corps that had swung around further to the north finally arrived to bolster the decimated Guards, and the German artillery weighed in, belatedly, but prevented a French counter-attack. The artillery commander was Felix's old friend Prince Kraft von Hohenlohe-Ingelfingen. After a ferocious battle, the French fell back, not only from St Privat but all along the line, and streamed back into Metz. The circle was closed around Bazaine and his five corps.

Busch broke the terrible news to Agnes three days after the battle. Minna's son Florentine, aged 18, was also killed in the first minutes of the attack, shot in the head. Agnes was devastated; all her premonitions had come true. Felix was gone and she had not been there to protect him. She now had to fulfil her sacred promise to Felix that if he were killed she would see that he was buried at Anholt. Everyone, including Prince Alfred, tried to dissuade her from attempting to recover the bodies of Felix and Florentine while hostilities were still in progress, but Agnes was not deterred. 'I would have gone to the grave of my poor Felix if I had had to walk on foot all the way.'

She, Miss Runkel and another lady in search of her son set out on a hospital train from Saarbrücken, headed for the Metz area. Alfred, who had had a change of heart, caught up with them just before they left. They reached Remilly, southeast of Metz, on 23 August. The place was jammed with troops and the wounded, and the only place they could find to stay was a railway car that held ample traces of the cattle and wounded soldiers it had carried. It was filthy. They managed to collect enough mattresses to cover the bottom of the car, and there Alfred, Busch, Agnes, Miss Runkel and others of the party spent the night. Two days later they were southwest of Metz at Ars-sur-Moselle, where Agnes browbeat a local man into making two zinc coffins for Felix and Florentine. He was afraid the French would hang him for making coffins for Prussian officers, but Agnes stood over him until he had finished the job.

Busch had found quarters in a large house with a garden in Jouy-aux-Arches, across the Moselle from Ars, and Agnes and her party soon joined him. On the twenty-seventh they had a family gathering there: Alfred and his two sons Leopold and Florentine, two members of another branch of the Salm family and Prince George Croÿ, a knight of Malta and a cousin.

The coffins were ready on the twenty-eighth, and Agnes set off in a cold rain for Ste Marie-aux-Chênes, from which the Guards had started their suicidal charge. Arriving at the badly damaged village, she met a Saxon lady, Frau Simon, who had gained much well-deserved fame for her tireless efforts to ameliorate the lot of the wounded. Despite opposition from conservative quarters, she always managed to be at the front with a well-trained body of nurses.

Agnes ripped into the Knights of St John, who placed obstacles in the way of nurses and voluntary sanitary associations that wished to be up front at the battlefields and not be bullied and treated with contempt by aristocratic snobs miles behind the lines. Soldiers whose wounds permitted them to be taken to depots in the rear received tolerably good treatment, but those who had to remain on the battlefield were sadly neglected. The death rate of battlefield amputees was dreadful, largely because they lacked food and water, or had to suffer rough transportation to the rear. Many of those who survived, opined Agnes, owed their lives to 'Mother Simon'.

The sanitary commissions and various religious orders, both Protestant and Catholic, normally took care of battlefield burials, but it was perforce a rough-and-ready business. For the most part, pits were dug and the bodies tumbled into them. The conditions of nineteenth-century warfare, with waves of men charging into the often withering fire of ever-more-lethal weapons, guaranteed horrific damage to man and horse alike. Corvin, among others, described the ghastly scene of the battlefields churned into mud by horses and artillery, soaked with blood and strewn with entrails, split skulls, shattered limbs and dead horses, all reeking of death. To add to the horror came the looters, usually hapless peasants from neighbouring villages seeking clothes or something of value, and not above finishing off any wounded they might find.

Frau Simon guided Agnes through the rain and mud to the mass grave where the officers of the Augusta Regiment had been buried. Felix and Florentine lay together in a rough coffin on top of the others, barely covered with earth. In what must have been a truly appalling moment for her, Agnes had the lid removed so that she could gaze once more on the beloved face of her husband. She saw only a putrefying black mass. She sank to the ground senseless. It had been a scant eight years since that happy day in Washington when she joined her life to that of the dashing Prussian prince.

With the aid of the kindly Frau Simon, she found a wagon to carry the coffins, and with only a knight of St John who agreed to accompany the sad cortege, she returned to Ars-sur-Moselle. Sanitary regulations required that the zinc coffins be enclosed in wooden cases. These were made while the grief-ridden Agnes waited. Despite wartime exigencies, the King put a special train at her disposal and, with Miss Runkel, she started for Anholt. They arrived on 2 September. Alfred stayed behind to be near his two sons.

The funeral service was held on 3 September with all the funeral pomp becoming the family. The two coffins were carried to the black-draped church and a high mass was celebrated. Among the mourners was Minna and Alfred's five daughters. Agnes wrote, 'Let me pass over details. It is too painful for me to dwell long on this sad period.'

Meanwhile, the reign of Emperor Napoleon III had come to an ignominious end. French Marshal MacMahon was ordered to the relief of Metz, but the German armies pushed him north toward the Belgian frontier. By 31 August, the dispirited and dis-organised French forces were crammed in and around the small fortress town of Sedan. With them was the ailing Emperor, driven to this last gesture by Empress Eugenie and the war party, who feared a revolution if he and the army fell back on Paris. The Germans snapped the trap shut, and on the late afternoon of 1 September Sedan capitulated. The next day the Emperor, MacMahon and 82,000 men passed into captivity. In five weeks, one French army had been imprisoned in Metz and another taken at Sedan. The way to Paris lay open.

The 3rd and 4th German Armies swept down on Paris, and had the city encircled by mid-September. The citizens, led by the newly constituted Government of National Defence, organised a heroic defence, but they suffered under constant bombardment (the artillery commander was, again, Prince Kraft von Hohenlohe-Ingelfingen) and mounting famine. So confident was Napoleon's government that France would win the war that it had made no effort to provision the city against a possible siege. Incredibly, the Government of National Defence, which had managed to escape Paris first for Tours and then Bordeaux, was able to raise and field army after army. The Germans had to fight every inch of the way as they strove to sweep up remaining French fortresses and consolidate their hold on the country.

The Queen Augusta Guards Regiment, reconstituted after the slaughter at St Privat, saw action again in a battle at the end of October at Le Bourget, northeast of Paris. Its commander, Count von Waldsee, had just rejoined the regiment after recovering from his St Privat wounds. The fighting was intense, and Waldsee was killed in the thick of it.

On 27 October Bazaine surrendered Metz and 173,000 French troops. The news caused fury in Paris, and he was accused of having sold the city. Agnes, who detested Bazaine for his actions in Mexico, got in her last word when she wrote,

> Though our religion teaches us that all bad actions are recorded and will find their punishment after death, it is always satisfactory if fate overtakes bad men in this life, and I regret that my poor husband did not live to see how Mexico and its noble Emperor were revenged on this bad, cruel, brutal and mean man, and his crafty master.

Bazaine was court-martialled in1873 and imprisoned, but he escaped and fled to Spain, where he died in 1888.

The capitulation of Metz freed up the German 2nd Army to move south toward Orléans on the Loire. The French were still a formidable foe, but the city fell finally on 4 December. The Germans kept defeating the French in open battle, but the French would not give up. The prolongation of the war and the logistical problems caused by the rapid German advance into France put great strains on the high command.

With its population driven to desperation by famine and constant bombardment, Paris finally capitulated on 28 January 1871. The Prussian high command had established its headquarters at Versailles in October 1870, and there on 18 January 1871 King

Wilhelm was proclaimed German Emperor. The date was not arbitrary: on 18 January 1701 the Elector of Brandenburg had been proclaimed King of Prussia. Wilhelm was actually quite reluctant to take this new title. He was first and foremost a Prussian, and he feared Prussia would be subordinated in the new German Empire. Given the ambitions of Bismarck, he need not have worried.

Agnes now made the critical decision to return to the war. The family wanted her to stay at Anholt, but, she wrote, 'I would have gone mad'. Only by throwing herself into the work she loved could she assuage her aching grief.

And throw herself she did. She was in her old element and, as always, was efficient and effective. She spent several days in Cologne collecting materiel needed in the field hospitals before Metz, and left for the front with three railway cars. The trip to Jouy-aux-Arches took eight days. She and Miss Runkel, and of course the terrier Jimmy who was still at her side, were billeted in Busch's house. Jimmy was older and a bit creaky, but still game.

Corvin was in the vicinity, and came to call. He did what he could to comfort Agnes, and they talked about happier days when the two couples had shared so many adventures. Corvin had always liked Felix despite his feckless ways, and he was deeply moved by the younger man's death. He agreed that work was the best medicine for Agnes.

Her first task was to organise kitchens for the five hospitals around Metz. They were crowded with sick and wounded, and the mess facilities were quite inadequate. She had trouble finding qualified nurses, for though there were many volunteers, they were for the most part 'voluntary nuisances, with their crinolines, plumed bonnets, and mincing manners'. They had no sense of discipline or punctuality, and took offence when asked to do anything they thought was demeaning – which was practically everything. Agnes predictably had absolutely no use for this set, and insisted on having sisters of mercy. She turned to Count Hompesch, a knight of Malta (and a descendant of Ferdinand von Hompesch, the order's last grand master in 1797), and he delivered almost at once. In no time a group of sisters of St Vincent de Paul arrived, and they were just what Agnes wanted: quiet, obedient and willing to do anything asked of them.

Baron Edward Oppenheim, who had helped her before, showed up with a load of mattresses, blankets, cots and assorted supplies Agnes had requested – bought and paid for by him. With this materiel as a foundation, Agnes established a depot into which poured donations from all over Germany.

Sometimes the donors of voluntary gifts wanted them to benefit the soldiers from their particular city or district. Thus those whose homes were near the Rhine were well supplied, while those from Pomerania, East and West Prussia or Silesia were neglected. When Agnes had sufficient general supplies, she tried to make up for this inequity. 'How well supplied my stores were, may be judged from the fact that I twice supplied a whole brigade of the second army corps – General von Fransecky's Pomeranians – with tobacco, cigars, and spirits.'

She still did a certain amount of hospital work, and assisted at operations, but her main task was – as in the Civil War – to procure and organise provisions. She had the invaluable support of Alfred and the indispensable Miss Runkel. Her work took her to many places around Metz, including Ste Marie-aux-Chênes of unhappy memory, where hospitals needed supplies.

When Dr Busch complained that there were not enough mattresses for the wounded in the hospitals, Agnes went straight to the top. Busch was only surgeon-general of the VIII Corps, and over him stood other authorities. The solution was to go to Steinmetz, 1st Army commander. He had encountered Agnes before, of course, and readily agreed to the measures she suggested for remedying the situation.

They watched the French army, now prisoners, march out of Metz after the capitulation of 27 October. With Metz in German hands, the hospitals were evacuated and the patients, both German and French, sent home. Agnes distributed clothes and supplies, and was gratified at their expression of thanks.

The 1st Army was ordered to move northwest to mop up French strong points in that direction. Steinmetz had come under intense criticism for the awful loss of life that attended his operations, and had been removed from command. Baron Edwin von Manteuffel replaced him.

It was time for Agnes to move on to new fronts, where there was much to be done. She was devastated by Felix's cruel death, but she could not and would not sit and weep. Agnes was made of sterner stuff. She had to keep working at what had become her mission – to bring care and solace to the sick and wounded. Agnes had always had a sympathetic streak for the unfortunate, and now that she was a widow, her desire to help was even stronger.

General von Manteuffel had begun his campaign in northern France, and the VIII Corps was part of his command. On 7 November 1870 Agnes, Alfred and Busch left Jouy with nine wagons and 18 horses. The cold was intense that winter, and dense fog and rains hampered movement. They headed for Brabant-en-Argonne, some 15 miles west of Verdun, where they found shelter in a shepherd's hut. Miss Runkel made coffee while Agnes cooked up some ham and eggs and Alfred brewed a hot whisky punch. 'Rather enjoying our strange situation, we sat on benches around the table, eating and drinking with a very good appetite.' As for sleeping, the men slept on straw on the floor while Agnes and Miss Runkel had the four-poster bed. They were almost asleep when the shepherdess came in with two nightcaps, 'for to sleep without a nightcap seems a preposterous idea to a Frenchwoman'.

Moving westward, they stopped one night in Vienne-le-Château, where the priest gave them a dinner that tasted something like chicken. Was it rabbit? No, cat! 'It was the first I ever ate, and I trust it was the last – though it was rather good. After all, such deceit from a clergyman grieved me.'

Some days later they were lodged in a chateau in a fine park belonging to one Baron Sachs.

> A gorgeously liveried footman opened the door of a saloon, announced with great emphasis, 'Madame la Princesse!' On entering we saw a fat old lady, Madame la Baronne de Sachs, dressed up like an English frigate on the birthday of the Queen, each of her fat fingers covered up to the third joint with sparkling rings, who looked rather perplexed when she saw two insignificant persons in black woolen dresses without any flounces...whom she probably took for two chambermaids preparing her for the arrival of Her Highness.

In the next ten days the party moved northwest, following the track of the 1st Army. On 19 November they were at Soissons, and on the twenty-first at Compiègne, where they remained for four days. They were quartered in a splendid villa, the owner of which was in besieged Paris, 'eating probably horse steaks and roast rats, whilst we were sitting at his sumptuously provided dinner table drinking Prussia's health in excellent French champagne'.

By now they had joined the staff of General von Goeben, commander of the VIII Corps, as the army moved on Amiens. In a dense fog on the twenty-seventh, near Moreuil, a small town just southeast of Amiens, the French launched a fierce attack and inflicted many casualties among their enemies. Agnes was all set to watch the battle, but a staff officer ordered her to take refuge behind a clump of bushes in a hollow, 'where we saw less than nothing'. In all of this she had with her the aged Jimmy and, of all things, a pet pigeon in a cage that she had acquired from somewhere. They were very near the hilltop command post of Manteuffel, who was somewhat nonplussed at their presence. The battle lasted all day, and they had not eaten since early morning, so they were cheered to be given some black bread and a slab of raw bacon. Amiens surrendered on the twenty-eighth and there were plenty of wounded there, in Moreuil and other towns for the team to succour. She and Busch drove to the nearby village of Boves, where there was a depot of the International Society, which provided supplies and materiel for the wounded. The terrible losses and suffering in the war excited great sympathy in Britain. Various agencies were formed in London to supplement the work of the sanitary commissions by sending medical stores, blankets, cots etc to aid the sick and wounded. The International Society was one of these. At the outbreak of the war, English sentiment was predominantly on the side of the Germans, but after the fall of the Second Empire, and with Paris enduring a terrible siege, opinion began to swing in favour of the French.

They found 12 wounded Germans and 200 wounded French, all under the care of French doctors, with whom they had correct but cordial discussions. An Englishman, Colonel Cox, was in charge of the International Society. He and his wife assisted Agnes liberally with what they had – and were to do so again later.

By 9 December they were in Rouen, which had fallen to the Prussians four days earlier. 'When we went out next day to look at the cathedral, we were struck by the appearance of the people, who stared at us with such burning hatred in their eyes that it was quite painful.' She called on Manteuffel and proposed an exchange of some 700 cigars she had for badly needed woollen clothes. The general was 'much amused with my talent for trade', and agreed to her terms.

They left Rouen to return to Amiens on the seventeenth, but ran into a battle south of the city, where the French had barred the road. General Louis Faidherbe had taken command of a new French army on 13 December, and moved north against Manteuffel's forces. Agnes and her party were within range of French fire, and were able to watch the German troops forming up for an attack. Seizing the moment, they found a little house on the road where they could set up a field hospital of sorts. The floor of one room they covered with straw for those who were fatally wounded and would die; in the other they set up tables for amputations.

Great numbers of gravely wounded men were brought in to them. Many were beyond help, with terrible abdominal wounds and massive internal bleeding that could not be stanched. There was nothing to do but make them as comfortable as possible and let them die. They were better off in a way than those whose limbs were shattered and were in constant and dreadful agony. Their cries and moans filled the little house.

The work and the horror were never-ending. While Busch amputated limbs, Agnes chloroformed the men and boiled water to wash off the blood and clean the wounds. She did what she could to sterilise the sponges, knives and other surgical instruments. Meanwhile, those soldiers who could walk kept bringing in more wounded. The house soon overflowed, and many men had to lie outside in the bitter cold until they could round up peasant carts to carry them jolting to Amiens. Agnes was greatly distressed to see the hapless amputees carried like sheep in these rough vehicles. She regretted the absence of the ambulances to which she had had recourse in America.

It was relentless, never-ending and exhausting work. And dangerous. While they toiled amidst the blood and dirt and the cries of the wounded, artillery shells were flying overhead and the unfortunate division pastor who was with them was seriously injured when he stepped outside for a bit of air and was hit by a bullet.

They had neither wine nor brandy for the wounded to help them against the cold. Cox of the International Society somehow found out about them, and in the nick of time sent them a wagonload of port wine, sherry, brandy, whisky, biscuits and condensed milk, as well as warm blankets and warm clothing.

After this long and terrible day, they went in the evening to Amiens, where all hands were needed to cope with the wounded. Agnes and Busch joined Miss Runkel, who had remained there. They worked steadily until three in the morning, when they fell onto their cots. They were up again at six, for renewed fighting was expected. And so the days went. Agnes never stopped. She tended the wounded, assisted at operations and amputations, comforted the dying, sent messages to wives and mothers, rounded up needed provisions.

The twenty-eighth of December was Felix's birthday, and Agnes's as well. It was the first time in eight years she had not been with him on that day, and was very cast down. To keep her mind off Felix, she worked all day in the hospital.

She did have one frightening experience. In a darkened room in a convent that was being used as a hospital she found a Frenchman crumpled on a cot. Coming closer, she saw that his face was black and backed quickly out of the room. Several days later she complained of a terrible headache and looked awful, her face red and inflamed. Busch took one look at her and announced that she had smallpox. She attributed her rapid recovery to her healthy blood, and the disease, if indeed it was smallpox, left only three little marks on her face. Busch insisted she stay in bed for four days, but on 16 January came marching orders for Peronne, east of Amiens up the Somme River. Busch said that she would die if she got up, but she brushed him off and marched on. The fields were covered with snow, and the freezing weather continued with no relief.

Two weeks earlier, a tenacious German defence had forced General Faidherbe to withdraw after a fierce battle near Péronne. Faidherbe made one last heroic effort, but on 19 January General August von Goeben (who had replaced Manteuffel) and the 1st

Army defeated him decisively at San Quentin. Agnes was called upon to establish yet another hospital, where she had some 500 patients to treat and feed. Miss Runkel worked herself into a state of collapse; Alfred found her lying senseless on the ground. Agnes had high praise for Alfred, who 'was untiring in his merciful duties as a knight of Malta; he was always on the spot day and night, and doing the most menial services in nursing not only the wounded but especially those with typhus or smallpox'. This was probably the high point in the relationship between Agnes and her brother-in-law. They had been comrades in adversity, and Alfred had never let his high rank keep him from his Christian duty.

After four dreadful months of siege, bombardment and famine, Paris capitulated on 28 January 1871. The armistice that followed provided for the surrender of all the forts remaining in French hands, for an indemnity of five billion francs and for general disarmament. The peace treaty signed on 28 February provided in addition for an army of occupation to remain until the indemnity had been paid and, perhaps the cruelest blow, for the cession to Germany of Alsace and much of Lorraine.

Many French commanders in the field, including Faidherbe, were incensed that the politicians had snapped the rug out from under them, but the game was up. The French were exhausted, the economy in shambles and its towns and cities in ruins. The bells rang out all over Germany, but its troops were as war-weary and exhausted as the French. The loss of life had hit hard. The war, which was to have been swift and surgical, had been anything but. The new German Empire had indeed triumphed, but at a cost. All in all the French lost 156,000 dead (17,000 of whom died of sickness and wounds as German prisoners) and 143,000 wounded and disabled. German casualties numbered 128,000 (24,000 dead, 89,000 wounded and 14,000 disappeared).

Busch and Agnes saw to the wrapping up of their medical responsibilities and, leaving their hospitals and clinics in what they hoped were capable hands, prepared to leave France. Felix's nephew Leopold, Alfred's eldest, came to escort her home, and so on 10 February, accompanied by Miss Runkel, Jimmy and the pet pigeon, Agnes set out to return to Schloss Anholt.

Manteuffel had recommended that the King – now Emperor – award her the Iron Cross, but that order, it was found, could be given only to men. Wilhelm therefore created a special decoration for women who had distinguished themselves during the war, the Verdienst-Kreuz or Distinguished Service Cross. Agnes was the first recipient. She was grateful, but she remarked that thousands of women qualified, whether at the front or in the rear lines.

She was also gratified to receive the following letter from Goeben:

> On your parting from here, [I] feel urged to express in the name of the 1st Army the thanks which the same owes to you. During all the war until peace, your Highness has with the utmost self-sacrifice uninterruptedly kept in view the difficult task which you undertook voluntarily at the commencement of the war, and which has benefited the sick and wounded in the most efficient manner. The army thanks you for this generous devotion from thousands of hearts, and as I now have the honour of commanding the 1st Army, I beg to be allowed to express to your Highness this thanks in the name of all, and especially of those whom the careful hand of your Highness has nursed and solaced in the hard days of suffering.

For three months since leaving Metz in November, Agnes had once again shown her mettle. The trials she endured while following the 1st Army on its sweep across northern France made anything she did in the Civil War pale by comparison. Now she was a professional, working beside one of the best surgeons in Germany. She had studied hard before the war broke out, and had ample opportunity to practice what she had learned. She never flinched at any hardship, and threw herself unstintingly into the awful work that had to be done. Compassionate, talented and tireless, she was a godsend to those with whom she worked and for those suffering wounded for whom she cared.

Her work was more than just a means to avoid thinking of Felix. This was her true calling, and she answered the call superbly. These months represented her finest hours.

EPILOGUE

The Later
Years

Alfred had preceded them to Schloss Anholt, and was there to welcome Agnes home. But it was not the same. Felix had joined all those ancestors whose portraits graced the great hall, as his was soon to do. The sole tie that bound Agnes Leclerq Joy to this ancient family had been severed.

For a few weeks she was content to rest on the lovely estate, far from the madness she had endured. She and Minna, bereaved at almost the same moment, drew close. They took long walks by the lake and along the streams in the great park that extended beyond the castle and consoled one another. Eventually, however, the future had to be faced. Agnes had to get on with her life.

Living at Schloss Anholt as a dependant of Alfred was clearly not an option. She was too independent. Besides, cracks now appeared in her relationship with her brother-in-law. They had worked tirelessly together in France, and Agnes had praised his dedication, but the 57-year-old prince had now resumed his role as lord of Anholt. The estates had to be put right after the disruptions of the war, and there were those ten children to be considered.

The main problem between them was the matter of Felix's debts, not only the old ones, but those incurred by the two of them while they lived a gay life in Coblenz.

Alfred had given Felix a generous allowance from his own pocket when he returned from Mexico, which had enabled him to pay off some of his debts. Felix's inheritance from his father had gone to pay off Austrian debts. He had been the beneficiary of certain other family- and estate-based income, but all these ceased at his death. Oddly, it seems that no provision existed for his widow. Worse, his life insurance policy was paid to Alfred. Whether this represented a failure on Felix's part to ensure Agnes's inheritance or some quirk in Prussian law, I cannot say, but the end result was that Agnes received no money whatsoever from Salm family sources.

Agnes felt strongly about the Coblenz debts that she and Felix had incurred. They were owed to servants and tradespeople, and she wanted to settle them. She had hoped, and expected, that her old comrade Alfred would come across with the funds she needed. He took instead a very hard line, insisted that she was not bound to pay them, and refused to lend her the money.

He did offer her lodging at Schloss Anholt, but she declined. She had a small pension as the widow of a Prussian major, and she had her pension from Emperor Franz Joseph, but these were barely enough to live on. Rather bitterly, she returned to her home in Coblenz with, she said, only about 200 thaler in her pocket. 'By his brave behavior in Mexico, and his glorious death, my poor husband had done more for the honour of his family than any of its members for several hundred years.' That the family would not now come up with a generous gesture she found unacceptable.

From here on, the Salm family seems to have dropped out of her life. In the pages of her book, she never mentioned them or Anholt again. Agnes had complained about the differences in wealth and status between her brother-in-law and her husband, and how the laws of Prussia favoured the former. When she had Felix, this shabby – she felt – treatment could be endured, but now it struck at her heart. One wonders, too, what Alfred and his aristocratic family and relations really thought of this unconventional American who had so bedazzled one of their own. They may have admired her courage, but she was not one of their kind. Indeed, they may have harboured some contempt for a woman who seemed so to relish getting her hands dirty. Agnes had criticised sharply the aristocratic ladies who were so useless in hospital duties, and the ladies undoubtedly resented her attitude.

It was a sad homecoming, despite the kindness of the regimental ladies and other friends. When she entered her home, her first, where she had had such a happy life with Felix, she was overwhelmed by memories. She went from room to room, picking up the little mementos they had collected on their travels. There was his writing desk, his clothes in their room – she was overwhelmed with grief and could not stop weeping.

Then, too, the creditors drove her to distraction, a situation made all the worse because she sympathised with most of them. One, however, was to cause her a great deal of trouble. He produced a bill with her signature, but it was an obvious forgery. The man took her to court. The court ultimately ruled in her favour, but she had to appear several times, and twice was obliged to interrupt her travels and return to Bonn.

She managed to borrow 2000 thaler from her old friend Baron Oppenheim, the Cologne banker, but more was needed. She decided that her only recourse was to go Berlin and ask for help from the Emperor. Wilhelm granted her an audience that lasted nearly an hour. He had always been friendly to Agnes, and he listened to her tale sympathetically. The upshot was that he arranged a generous loan of 4000 thaler, but she had to repay it in annual instalments. This incident points up once again the extraordinary effect Agnes could have on important people. Again and again they came through for her, however exalted their stature.

Empress Augusta offered her a place in the Augusta Hospital, a very elaborate and elegantly appointed facility designed to offer accommodations for sick persons unable to pay for board and treatment. The royal benefactress had also recruited the daughters of impecunious titled families, who could by their work benefit society and at the same time find protection from care and want. All very well, thought Agnes, but things would go a lot better at the hospital were sisters of charity substituted for the noble nurses.

She spent two weeks at the Augusta Hospital before returning to Coblenz. Memories of the past and the remaining insistent debtors wore her down, so she decided to move to Bonn for a change of scene. She rented a house there, and cleaned out the apartment in Coblenz. But she was not well and, on top of all else, had to suffer through several lawsuits brought by debtors. Though the courts ruled in her favour, the whole process was debilitating.

The doctor advised Switzerland, so off she went to Lucerne, incognito as Baroness Stein, with Miss Runkel, who agreed to accompany her. Her health improved, but she was overcome with sadness. Trying to shake it off, she decided she must try to find a hospital to manage, or if that did not work out, enter a convent.

What she apparently did not consider was returning to America. Her ties there were minimal and, despite all her problems, she was still Princess zu Salm-Salm. She had many friends at the apex of a grand society in which she had become accustomed to move. It was a gay, glittering society, and America in her mind paled by comparison. More practically, she needed her two pensions, and these would cease if she moved back to the US where she had no prospects at all. It was too much of a gamble.

After two months in Lucerne she returned to Bonn, where Oppenheim had in the meantime managed to satisfy most creditors, but others both false and real continued to clamour. Her health declined anew, and in October 1872 she went to a pension in Clarens on Lake Geneva, near Montreux, where she passed a peaceful and agreeable life till after Christmas. With the cold, her ailments increased and the doctors recommended Italy.

She picked up at this prospect, and went to Pisa, taking Miss Runkel and Jimmy with her. I suspect that Miss Runkel was now a companion in the formal sense of the word, helping Agnes cope with loneliness. They found cheap and agreeable lodgings in the house of a doctor. The local priest tutoring her in Italian discovered he had a princess on his hands, and the news soon spread, so she was scooped up by society. She found the company very agreeable and her spirits improved.

Mount Vesuvius erupted and, being Agnes, she had to see it. Off to Naples and up the ash-covered mountain she went, with, of course, Miss Runkel and Jimmy. The authorities had established a safety line, but Agnes insisted on going on, jumping chasms. Miss Runkel stayed behind, holding Jimmy, but the dog got away and ran after Agnes. He burned his feet on hot stones, so she had to carry him.

We returned, however, without incident to the place where the rest of the company had remained, and refreshed ourselves with a bottle of Lachrymae Christi, regretting very much that the vineyard where it had been grown was covered several feet deep with ashes from which the tops of the vines scarcely peeped out.

It was the old Agnes again.

She now began to consider seriously the notion of entering a convent. Agnes had probably become Catholic to marry Felix, but she had lived among Catholics now for some years, and found the faith comforting and a source of much-needed solace. In her present loneliness, the Church seemed even more attractive. Then, too, she observed, life in a convent would be a lot less expensive for her. So, with typical industry, she set her sights on Pope Pius IX. She needed introductions, and pulled those strings she had. From Empress Augusta she got a letter to an important figure at the papal court, and from Oppenheim one to the German minister in Rome.

After some manoeuvring, her request for an audience was granted. Pope Pius received her kindly, but told her he did not think she had the vocation for a nunnery. He advised her to reflect on the matter for another year to see whether she would change her mind. 'This advice of the Holy Father was extremely kind; his clear mind anticipated what would happen; he read my character, for indeed I changed my mind, and before the year had passed I did not think any more of burying myself in a nunnery.'

She availed herself of her contacts to move about in Roman society, meet all sorts of people and have a second audience with the Pope. They must have discussed Mexico. Pius had been outraged by the anti-clerical reform laws passed by the Mexican government in 1857, and threatened to excommunicate anyone who took the oath to obey them. He had also had a rather rocky time with Carlota when she insisted on staying overnight in the Vatican, claiming that Napoleon III's agents were trying to poison her. He let her stay one night. At the time of Agnes's visit, Pius was living as the 'prisoner of the Vatican'. The new kingdom of Italy had occupied and annexed Rome in 1870, abolishing the Papal States. Perhaps Agnes was a welcome distraction for the harassed pontiff.

Her confessor, Father Mullooly, an Irish Dominican, was another interesting man. He was prior of the Church of San Clemente, a most unusual church which is still in the hands of the Irish fathers. Father Mullooly, in fact, began the excavations in 1857 that revealed the ancient churches below the present one, back to the earliest days of Christianity. Agnes was fascinated by San Clemente.

> The fresco pictures are highly interesting, and as their subterranean wonders have been accessible only since 1866, many visitors to Rome will scarcely know anything of them, and artists and antiquarians who should happen to read my book will thank me for having drawn their notice to St. Clement.

Her pleasant stay in Rome was interrupted after five weeks by the necessity of returning to Bonn to make a personal appearance at court in connection with that troublesome forgery lawsuit.

That over, she was invited by friends to stay with them in Rostock, on the Baltic Sea, capital of the Grand Duchy of Mecklenburg-Schwerin (which, with its sister duchy of Mecklenburg-Strelitz, was one of the few north German states to escape absorption by Prussia). The Grand Duchess Dowager, mother of the reigning Grand Duke, was a sister of Emperor Wilhelm. They had met at Bad Ems, so Agnes (once again) had an entrée right at the top. In no time at all Agnes was presented to Grand Duke Friedrich Franz II and his spouse. The success of Agnes's sojourn in Rostock was assured, and she had a grand time. They went to the spa of Warnemunde on the Baltic for the annual water festival that was always attended by the grand ducal court. Several hundred boats decked out with garlands of flowers, fanciful canopies and Chinese lanterns sailed down the Warne River with the court up front. There was music, a battle of bouquets and much gaiety.

Once again that irritating forgery suit interrupted her pleasures, and again she had to return to Bonn. Her health failed again, and she had fainting spells and an overwhelming weakness. To recover, she went to the seashore at Scheveningen, on the Dutch coast near the Hague. But she was very depressed.

In the past, and during the late war, her natural energy and drive had carried her through many difficult times. She had not allowed fatigue and worry to overcome her. She had to keep going for herself and for Felix, even though he was no longer by her side. But now it was very different. To the fatigue and anxieties of the past had been added what she characterised as the 'humiliations and mortifications' she had suffered at the hands of Alfred. Her deep loneliness was made worse by her constant financial worries. Her limited income imposed restrictions on her movements; she could not keep up with the society to which she had become accustomed. A dark cloud had settled on her life, and she was not able to shake it loose.

At this dark moment, Agnes was unexpectedly saved. Her angel was still on duty.

She received news at Scheveningen that a distant relative whom she had not seen or heard of since childhood had died and left her a comfortable legacy. He had been very fond of Agnes when she was a lively child, and had kept up with her adventures in the newspapers – the marriage to a prince, the Civil War, her exploits in Mexico – and had made over to his bank a substantial sum of which she was to receive the interest.

This tiny glimpse into her past, with a kindly relative being fond of her, makes one wonder if her childhood was as bleak as rumoured.

A goodly sum was at once placed at her disposal, and she immediately purchased the house in Bonn that she had been renting. She let it to Gerolt, her old friend from Washington, whom Bismarck had recalled from his post as minister in 1871 after 25 years. There had been a dispute over policy and Agnes thought Gerolt had been treated unfairly. She was glad to repay the old man's past kindness to them.

Winter was setting in, and Agnes decided to go south, to Spain. The ever-faithful Miss Runkel wanted to return to her family. It seems that marriage beckoned. She and Agnes had been through a great deal together. Agnes was not only very fond of the younger woman, but admired her capacity for hard work. She had been a great comfort to Agnes on many occasions.

But she had her own life to lead, and Agnes was obliged to let her go.

By a stroke of luck, a friend from the German legation in Rome was now with the embassy in Madrid, and through him she found excellent lodgings. She took in the sights, including the Prado, where she went often to admire the collection. She was rebuffed when she tried to visit the palace of the dukes of Osuna, but when she established that the current duchess, Eleanor, was both a friend and her husband's first cousin, she was admitted with alacrity and low bows. 'It is a splendid dwelling, and I admired much the order in which it was kept by the creditors of the duke, who had taken possession of the palace.' She must have sympathised. The bulk of the duke's great fortune, she explained, was tied up in landed property in Andalucia, and owing to the unsettled political conditions of Spain, the fields were not tilled and taxes were not paid.

Back in Bonn, she settled down to finish her book. It was published in Stuttgart in 1875. Her final paragraph reads,

> In taking leave of the kind readers who may perhaps be interested in my fortunes, I beg to say that I have at last found that rest for which I longed so much. I have a home with which I am perfectly satisfied, am independent in every respect, and have some true friends who know and love me; more I do not desire.

And settle down she did, to enjoy the windfall that had so fortuitously come her way. She retrieved her house in Bonn from Gerolt, who did not long survive his recall from Washington. Bonn was an attractive small town on the Rhine midway between Coblenz and Cologne. Agnes loved the Rhineland, with its busy river traffic, the castles perched on crags, the vineyards spilling down the steep sun-drenched slopes. With all her connections she led a pleasant social life. Felix was gone, and she had no further ties with Anholt, but Agnes was a charming woman who had made a favourable impression on many important people, and she could certainly stand on her own two feet. She was also a war widow, and there were many others like her to support each other in many ways.

Agnes was, however, an attractive woman, still only in her mid-thirties. At some point she must have decided it was time to put an end to her loneliness. She began to keep a sharp lookout at the social functions she attended. Somewhere along the way, she met Charles Heneage (1841–1901), a British diplomat accredited to Karlsruhe, capital of the Grand Duchy of Baden. Grand Duchess Louise was a daughter of Emperor Wilhelm and Empress Augusta, and Agnes had known her and her consort for several years, so she would have been a familiar in Karlsruhe circles. Heneage was her age and come from a reasonably well-to-do and well-placed family (his older brother was created Baron Heneage in 1896). They were married in the Protestant church in Coblenz in September 1876.

Note, the Protestant church. After 14 years as a Catholic, Agnes returned to the Protestant fold. She had become a Catholic for the sake of Felix; she resumed her original faith to marry Charles. I suspect that she took a rather relaxed view of faith anyway; she was as God-fearing as the next person, but she did not trouble too much about the details. The repercussions in her social set must have been profound. Her Catholic lady friends were no doubt scandalised. Religion was not a matter taken lightly in Europe, which had suffered more than its share of religious wars in the past. The marriage also took place in the midst of Bismarck's *Kulturkampf*, or cultural struggle. The new German Empire was determined to subordinate all groups within the state to its sovereign power, and it thus clashed head-on with the desire of the Papacy to control its hierarchy. The loss of Rome and the Papal States to Italy in 1870 only hardened Pius IX's resolve to strengthen the spiritual power and influence of the Church. Bismarck would have none of this, and in a series of laws reined in the Catholic hierarchy in Germany.

This was, then, a sensitive time for Agnes to leave the Catholic Church. Her conversion and remarriage also brought an end to any thought of reconciliation with the Salm family.

For whatever reason, her marriage to Heneage did not last. She did, however, go with her husband to England, where they lived for a while, long enough for Agnes to precipitate a crisis of protocol. The archives at Schloss Anholt preserve a letter written to *The Star* by Heneage on 30 June 1899, apparently in answer to an earlier article, in which he explains that Agnes found herself in a curious position when she married him. English law recognised her as a princess, but not as a 'Serene Highness' ('Durchlaucht'), her title in Germany. She was also, he wrote, 'debarred from wearing her foreign orders won by personal bravery on the field of battle, nursing the wounded under fire'. Heneage managed to have this anomaly brought to the attention of Queen Victoria in 1887. On the advice of Lord Salisbury, the prime minister, the Queen permitted Agnes to wear her decorations in England and at foreign courts, and to retain her title of 'Princess', but without Serenity. Trust Agnes to get the highest powers in the land involved in her affairs. The foreign orders were the San Carlos of Mexico, bestowed on her by Maximilian, and her two German orders, the Verdienst Kreuz and the Kriegsmünze. When asked her affiliations at one point, she admitted to being a bit confused: an American, widow of a German, married to an Englishman.

In 1892 she invited her 11-year old nephew Frederick Johnson, sister Delia's youngest son, to live with her in Bonn and attend school there. He was with her for five years before returning to his family in New Jersey. Frederick was the younger brother of the Felix whom Agnes had 'adopted' all those years ago in Georgia but who apparently never entered her life again. Was Agnes suffering another pang of regret for her childlessness? Or did she simply feel that Frederick, who was in delicate health, could receive better care in Germany than at home? The incident points up Agnes's continued attachment to Delia and her family – alone among her siblings.

The decade of the 1880s saw the deaths of a number of her friends. Dr Busch, from whom she had learned so much and with whom she had shared so much, went in 1881. Prince Karl Anton von Hohenzollern, who had been very kind and helpful to Felix and Agnes, followed in 1885. The next year brought another grievous loss. Corvin, who had been a friend from her earliest days with Felix and had seen her often in Germany, died in 1886. He had been living in Rorschach, Switzerland, which he had come to love in his days there with the Salms. His book *In France with the Germans* was written in Rorschach. Emperor Wilhelm I came to the end of his reign in 1888, and Empress Augusta lived but two more years. With their going, the whole atmosphere of the court Agnes had found so congenial changed dramatically.

Their son, the liberal-minded Friedrich III, reigned for three short months before succumbing to cancer. His successor was Wilhelm II, cast from a very different mold. These and other deaths must have saddened Agnes greatly; those who had known and loved her and Felix were slowly disappearing.

From Schloss Anholt came news of Minna's death in 1887. Felix's cousin Eleanor, Duchess of Osuna, went in 1891. Alfred died in 1896, to be succeeded by his son Prince Leopold. He was not in the best of health, and died childless in 1908. From his brother and successor, another Alfred, descends the present head of the family, Prince Carl Philipp.

The outbreak of the Spanish–American War in April 1898 brought Agnes out of retirement. She went to London to organise an Anglo–American ambulance corps, but the war was over before she could do much.

In the spring of 1899, she went to New York to return the flags of the 8th and 68th New York Volunteer Regiments that Felix had taken to Germany. This was her first visit to the US since she had sailed for Germany in 1867. That the mystery of her origin persisted is indicated by an article in the *New York Herald* of 4 March announcing the impending arrival of Princess Salm-Salm, the daughter of a French planter in Cuba. She arrived that day, and the *Herald* of the fifth enthused, 'An auburn haired, bright eyed, jolly little woman is the Princess Salm-Salm of Bonn, who arrived yesterday on the steamship *Kaiser Wilhelm der Grosse*'. She visited her sister Delia and her family in Vineland, in southern New Jersey, and it was reported that a brilliant reception was planned for her in Washington DC. *The Times* described her as 'slender, of medium height, and her hair is more auburn than gray. She has a bright pleasant face with sparkling eyes.' In response to questions, Agnes denied that she had ever thought of going on the stage, that she had fallen from a tight rope in Chicago and that she had once ridden down Pennsylvania Avenue, Washington, in the uniform of a captain.[6] This is the only known occasion when she commented on her past and the rumours surrounding her origins.

The return of the battle flags on 14 May 1899 was an impressive event. Agnes had written to New York Governor Theodore Roosevelt about her plans, and he heartily concurred. The ceremony was held at Kaplan's Odd Fellows Hall on East 8th Street, at the time the centre of the German community in New York. It was well covered by the New York press. The *New York Journal* and the *New Yorker Staats-Zeitung* ran sketches of Agnes wearing all her decorations and a great riband across her bosom. She was dressed, wrote the *New York Times*, 'in a black silk gown with a long train and a small black hat fringed with pink roses. There was a red ribbon over her shoulder, and on her breast were medals of gold that had been presented to her for bravery on the field of battle.'[7]

The *New York Journal* reported that she was 'a woman of fine presence', and after describing her attire and her medals noted, 'She had epaulets on her shoulders and altogether made a military appearance'.[8]

The date was not chosen arbitrarily. Thirty-eight years before, on 14 May 1861, Mayor Fernando Wood had presented the flags to the regiment on the steps of City Hall. They had been given by the banker August Belmont, born in the Rhineland, as were so many of the regiment. The 8th marched off to battle 1040 strong; 168 returned. Twenty-nine veterans turned out for the ceremony with family and friends, along with a small contingent of the old 68th, for a total of some 250 people. As Agnes and entourage entered the hall and proceeded toward the podium, the band struck up 'Ich hatte ein Kameraden'. The Johnsons were there, and various Joy relatives, including Representative Charles T. Joy of Missouri, Julius Stahel, the last living colonel of the 8th, and Mrs Caroline Belmont, widow of the recently deceased August (and a daughter of Commodore Matthew Perry). 'The lady had a friendly word and a winning smile for all,' wrote the *Staats-Zeitung*.

After suitable speeches, Agnes presented the flags to George Grothe, Commander of the Blenker Veterans Association. She had flags also for the few veterans of the 68th who had gathered. The last to speak was probably the most distinguished person there. General Carl Schurz went into politics after the Civil War. He was US senator from Missouri (1869–75) and Secretary of the Interior (1877–81) under President Hayes. He arose to thunderous applause, reported the *Staats-Zeitung*, and told how he had seen the 8th fight at both Bull Runs and at Chancellorsville.

He had also seen them at Harrisonburg in the Shenandoah Valley of Virginia after the harrowing march across country when Blenker's Brigade was lost. Missing from the party was old Franz Sigel, former commander of the XI Corps of the Army of the Potomac, who was ill (he died in 1902), but sent regrets and best wishes. The ceremony concluded with a banquet, and was pronounced a great success by all.[9]

In October 1899 the South African War broke out, and Agnes stood front and centre again. She wanted to take charge of an ambulance. She was warned of hardships, but was quoted as responding, 'Hardships have no terror for me. I know well what they mean.'[10] One can only wonder about her political judgment, though. While in London to collect funds, she cabled President Paul Kruger of the Transvaal, the Boer leader against whom the British were fighting, asking his permission to serve as a nurse. The British censors in Aden intercepted her telegram. As ever, Agnes had no interest in the politics of the situation. There was a war on, and she wanted to help. Significantly, she wanted to help the Boers, with whom Germany sympathised.

Though she was optimistic about raising funds in Europe for an ambulance corps, something went wrong and they never materialised. In February 1900 she returned to the US to launch an appeal, and the *New York Herald* of 16 February 1900 reported that she was in town to organise an ambulance corps for the Boer army. At least $30,000 was needed to equip a corps with a hundred beds, several ambulances etc. The paper noted that she had cabled Clara Barton, founder of the American Red Cross, in Washington, asking for a meeting. Agnes was a member of the German Red Cross, and she told the reporter, 'I am going there to aid the Boer sick and wounded, but I will not discriminate between Boers and Englishmen'. She added, 'This will make my fourth war, and when it is over I will bring out a final edition of my book'.

Her efforts were apparently in vain. The *New York Times* of 2 April 1900 reported that she had given up trying to raise funds for an ambulance corps, and was going to start a fund for Boer widows and orphans. A couple of weeks later the paper noted that she was selling tickets in Wall Street for a benefit concert. She sailed for Europe on 11 May after a lavish farewell dinner at the

Hotel Manhattan in New York attended by a host of dignitaries. She was not to return. Her home was now in Bonn.

There is something rather sad in Agnes's efforts to become involved again with helping the victims of war. She had done so much in her day, but the world had moved on by three decades, and new people and techniques had come along. She was – one hesitates to guess – no longer relevant.

About 1903, she moved to Karlsruhe, where she lived out quietly the years remaining to her. She had an apartment on the first floor of Karlstrasse 2, where she died on 21 December 1912. Her obituary appeared in the *Karlsruher Zeitung* of 24 December. It gave a reasonably accurate account of her and her life with Felix. The article reflects a slight shading of her age, though, for it has her born in 1844 rather than 1840.

The following day the *Karlsruhe Zeitung* carried the following brief notice. 'On Monday at midday took place the cremation of Princess Salm-Salm, according to her wishes, in the company of a small circle of her friends and in a simple ceremony. Pastor Stöckle of Münster preached a deeply moving sermon ['eine tiefempfundene Trauerrede'].' Would that his words had been preserved.[11]

The *New York Times* of 22 December 1912 noted that Princess Agnes Salm-Salm had died in Karlsruhe the previous day, and went on to say, 'The former American actress was a nurse in the Franco–Prussian War'. She was born in Baltimore, the daughter of an American colonel named Leclerq, and married Prince Felix Salm-Salm, 'a soldier of fortune'. In the Franco–Prussian War she served as a hospital nurse and was decorated for bravery. Agnes would not have been pleased being remembered as an actress.

She was buried in the Protestant cemetery in Karlsruhe. Felix and Schloss Anholt were by now too far away and across a religious divide. She did, however, bequeath to Felix's family a white marble bust of Felix which she had commissioned. It stands now in a corridor of Schloss Anholt, alone and rather cold.

It is rather unsatisfactory for the author and presumably for the reader that Agnes seems gradually to fade from view the last decades of her life. One would have preferred to have her exit to thunderous applause, on horseback of course, with a great red plume or a long blue veil floating from her tall stylish hat.

But she had done all that. She had had an extraordinary life, going from a high-wire act in a circus in Chicago to dining with royalty. Along the way, she had dealings with two presidents of the US, one emperor and one president of Mexico, a king and queen of Prussia who became the German emperor and empress, and one pope, not to mention grand dukes, dukes, princes and other members of the European aristocracy, senators, governors, generals, diplomats and statesmen of several nations. And when she talked to them, she looked them straight in the eye and they usually did what she wanted of them.

But the most important part of her legacy, perhaps, is her hospital work. Under occasionally the most frightful conditions, she served the sick, the wounded and the desperate, and served them with skill and compassion. Her heart went out to the unfortunate, be they the war-shocked citizens of the south during the Civil War or the Indians of Mexico, still suffering from the cruelties of the Spanish conquest, or the wounded French she as a Prussian nurse tended to during the Franco–Prussian War.

If she chose to avoid the limelight during the last years of her life, she deserved the peace and quiet. She had been famous in her day, and the fact that the *New York Times* reported her death in 1912, 12 years after her last visit to the US, indicates that her fame had lingered on. I hope this book is a suitable tribute to a truly remarkable woman.

Notes on the Text

Notes on Part I

1   *New York Herald*, 9 April 1899, Sec. 4, 5.

2   Noah Brooks, 'The Career of an American Princess', *Overland Monthly and Outwest Magazine*, vol. 5 no 5, November 1870, p. 461.

3   Brooks, p. 463.

4   Baron Friedrich Otto von Fritsch, *A Gallant Captain of the Civil War* (New York, c.1902), p. 114.

5   Wilhelm Kaufmann, *Die Deutschen im amerikanischen Bürgerkriege* (Munich, 1911), p. 172.

6   Kaufmann, p. 180.

7   George B. McClellan, *McClellan's Own Story* (New York, 1887), pp. 141–42.

8   Margaret Leech, *Reveille in Washington, 1860–1865* (New York, 1941), paperback edn (Alexandria, VA, 1962), p. 17.

9   Otto von Corvin, *In France with the Germans* (London, 1872), vol. 1, pp. 10–13.

10   Brooks, p. 464.

11   Charles S. Wainwright, *The Personal Journals of Col. Charles S. Wainwright, 1861–65*, ed. Allen Nevins (New York, 1962), p. 175.

12   Brooks, p. 465.

13   Thomas Keneally, *American Scoundrel* (New York, 2002), p. 263.

14   *War of the Rebellion: Official Records of the Union and Confederate Armies* (Washington, 1880 on), I, 51, pt 1, p. 998.

15   Fritsch, p. 106. Subsequent quotations from Fritsch are from pp. 106–25, passim.

16   A brevet usually conferred a rank in the army as a whole one step above what he had held in his regiment or corps. It was used to reward meritorious conduct, and during the Civil War hundreds of brevet commissions were bestowed, causing great confusion. The practice fell into disuse after 1865, being replaced by the system of decorations, and was abolished in 1922.

17   D. S. Stanley, *The Memoirs of Maj. Gen. David S. Stanley* (Cambridge, MA, 1917), p. 191.

18   *War of the Rebellion*, I, 45, pt 1, pp. 514–19.

19 This and the preceding telegrams are in AGO, M-1064, Roll 215
    1863, S-396.
20 Franklin M. Garrett, *Atlanta and Environs: A Chronicle of Its People
    and Events* (Athens, GA), I, p. 681.

Notes on Part II

1   As with Agnes's book, I have not footnoted the many quotes from
    Felix's diary.
2   Henry B. Parkes, *A History of Mexico* (Boston, 1960), p. 244.
3   Albert Hans, *Queretaro: Souvenir d'un officier de l'Empereur Maximilian*
    (Paris, 1869), p. 107.
4   Hans, *Queretaro*, p. 142.
5   Count Egon Caesar Corti, *Maximilian and Carlota of Mexico*, 2 vols
    (New York, 1928), p. 795.
6   Hans, *Queretaro*, p. 199.
7   Mariano Escobedo, *Documentos*, ed. Masao Sugawara (Mexico City,
    1987), Document 196, pp. 413ff.
8   José Luis Blasio, *Maximiliano Íntimo* (Paris/Mexico, 1905), p. 376.
9   This supposed connection, which is mentioned by others, is prob-
    ably due to some confusion with Agnes's brother-in-law Edmund
    Johnson.
10 *New York Herald*, 11 June 1867, p. 7.
11 Frederic Hall, *Life of Maximilian I, Late Emperor of Mexico* (New York,
    1868), p. 208.
12 José Fuentes Mares, *Juárez y el Imperio* (Mexico, 1963), p. 232.
13 Samuel Basch, *Erinerungen aus Mexico* (Leipzig, 1868), p. 198.
14 Jasper Ridley, *Maximilian and Juárez* (New York, 1992), p. 277.
15 *New York Herald*, 24 July 1867, p. 10.
16 Felix's *Diary*, vol. II, covers his captivity and contains other rele-
    vant documents.
17 *New York Herald*, 10 November 1867, p. 9.
18 Frederick W. Seward, *Seward at Washington* (New York 1891), vol. 3,
    p. 366.
19 *New York Herald*, 29 November 1867, 3.
20 Ulick Ralph Burke, *A Life of Benito Juarez* (London, 1894), p. 321.

Notes on Part III

1   Corvin, pp. 15–16.
2   Corvin, p. 22.
3   Corvin, p. 69.
4   Philipp Elliot-Wright, *Gravelotte–St Privat 1870* (London, 1993), pp. 77–78.
5   Michael Howard, *The Franco–Prussian War* (New York, 1961), p. 175.
6   *New York Times*, 5 April 1899, 1.
7   *New York Times*, 15 May 1899, 3.
8   *New York Journal*, 15 May 1899, under the heading 'Sacred Battle Flags Restored'.
9   The longest account of the ceremony appeared in the *New Yorker Staats-Zeitung* of 15 May 1899, but the *New York Times*, *New York Herald* and *New York Journal* of the same date also carried stories.
10 *New York Herald*, 10 December 1899.
11 I am indebted to Dr Ludger Syré of the Baden State Library in Karlsruhe for the two articles from the *Karlsruhe Zeitung* about Agnes, as well as for her address at Karlstrasse 2, first floor.

Bibliography

The two fundamental sources for the Salms' story are their books:

Salm-Salm, Princess Agnes, *Ten Years of My Life* (London, 1876), originally published in German (Stuttgart, 1875); also Detroit, 1877.

Salm-Salm, Prince Felix, *My Diary in Mexico in 1867 including the Last Days of the Emperor Maximilian with Leaves from the Diary of the Princess Salm-Salm*, 2 vols (London, 1868), originally published in German (Stuttgart, 1868). The second volume of the *Diary* covers his captivity and release.

The Civil War

Brooks, Noah, *Mr Lincoln's Washington* (South Brunswick, NJ, 1967).

Brooks, Noah, 'The Career of an American Princess,' *Overland Monthly and Outwest Magazine* (San Francisco), vol. 5, no 5, November 1870.

Burton, William L., *Melting Pot Soldiers: The Union's Ethnic Regiments* (New York, 1998).

Carmichael, Flossie, and Ronald Lee, *In and Around Bridgeport* (Collegedale, TN, 1969).

Coffey, David, 'Prince Felix and Princess Agnes Salm-Salm', in Woodworth, Steven E. (ed.), *The Human Tradition in the Civil War and Reconstruction* (Wilmington, DE, 2000).

Davis, William C., *Lincoln's Men* (New York, 1999).

Donald, David, *Lincoln* (New York, 1995).

Dyer, Frederick, *A Compendium of the War of the Rebellion* (New York, 1908; new edition, 1994).

Foote, Shelby, *The Civil War*, 3 vols (New York, 1986).

Fritsch, Friedrich Otto, Baron von, *A Gallant Captain of the Civil War, being the record of the extraordinary adventures of Friedrich Otto, Baron von Fritsch, compiled from his war record in Washington and his private papers*, ed. and compiled by Joseph Tyler Butts (New York, c. 1902).

Garrett, Franklin M., *Atlanta and Environs: A Chronicle of Its People and Events* (Athens, GA, 1969).

Groom, Winston, *Shrouds of Glory: from Atlanta to Nashville* (New York, 1995).

Joy, James R., *Thomas Joy and his Descendents* (New York, 1900).

Kaufmann, Wilhelm, *Die Deutschen im amerikanischen Bürgerkrieg* (Munich, 1911).

Keneally, Thomas, *American Scoundrel: The Life of … General Dan Sickles* (New York, 2002).

Kurtz, Annie, 'Prince Who Ruled Atlanta', *Atlanta Journal/Constitution*, 14 January, 1934.

Leech, Margaret, *Reveille in Washington, 1860–1865* (Alexandria, VA, 1962; originally published 1941).

Lonn, Ella, *Foreigners in the Union Army and Navy* (Baton Rouge, LA, 1951).

McClellan, George B., *McClellan's Own Story* (New York, 1887).

Official Army Register of the Volunteer Forces of the US Army, 1861–65, 8 vols.

Pfisterer, Frederick, *New York in the War of the Rebellion, 1861 to 1865* (Albany, NY, 1912; originally published 1890).

Rosengarten, J. G., *The German Soldier in the Wars of the United States* (Philadelphia, 1890).

Schrader, Frederick F., *The Germans in the Making of America* (Boston, 1924).

Schurz, Carl, *The Reminiscences of Carl Schurz* (New York, 1908).

Sears, Stephen, *Chancellorsville* (New York, 1996).

Stanley, David S., *The Memoirs of Major David S. Stanley* (Cambridge, MA, 1917).

Wainwright, Charles S., *The Personal Journals of Col. Charles S. Wainwright, 1861–65* (New York, 1962).

War of the Rebellion: Official Records of the Union and Confederate Armies (Washington, 1880 on).

Warner, Ezra J., *Generals in Blue* (Baton Rouge, LA, 1964).

Zucker, A. E., *The Forty-Eighters* (New York, 1950).

Mexico

Basch, Samuel, *Erinerungen aus Mexico* (Leipzig, 1868).

Blasio, José Luis, *Maximiliano Íntimo* (Paris/Mexico, 1905).

Burke, Ulick Ralph, *A Life of Benito Juarez* (London, 1894).

Corti, Count Egon Caesar, *Maximilian and Carlota of Mexico*, 2 vols (New York, 1928; originally published in German, Zürich, 1924).

Escobedo, Mariano, *Documentos*, ed. Masao Sugawara (Mexico City, 1987).

Fuentes Mares, José, *Juárez y el Imperio* (Mexico City, 1963).

Hall, Frederic, *Life of Maximilian I, Late Emperor of Mexico* (New York, 1868).

Hans, Albert, *Queretaro: Souvenir d'un offcier de l'Empereur Maximilian* (Paris, 1869).

Martin, Percy F., *Maximilian in Mexico* (New York, 1914).

Niles, Blair, *Passengers to Mexico* (New York, 1943).

Parkes, Henry B., *A History of Mexico* (Boston, 1960).

Pedrazo, José Francisco, *Juárez en San Luis Potosí* (San Luis Potosí, 1972).

Pitner, Ernst, *Maximilian's Lieutenant* (Alburquerque, NM/London, 1993).

Ridley, Jasper, *Maximilian and Juárez* (New York, 1992).

Riva Palacios, Mariano, and Rafael Martínez de la Torre, *Memorandum sobre el processo del Archiduque Fernando Maximiliano de Austria* (Mexico, 1867).

Seward, Frederick H., *Seward at Washington*, vol. 3 (New York, 1891).

Smissen, le Général Baron van der, *Souvenirs de Méxique, 1864–1867* (Brussels, 1892).

Germany

Baedeker, Karl, *Les Bords du Rhin* (Coblenz, 1870).
— The Rhine from Rotterdam to Constance (1903).
— Switzerland (1881).
Cassell's History of the Franco–German War (London, 1895).
Corvin, Otto von, *In France with the Germans*, 2 vols (London, 1872).
Deutsche Biographische Enzyklopädie (Munich, 1995).
Elliot-Wright, Philipp, *Gravelotte–St Privat 1870* (London, 1993).
Eyck, Erich, *Bismarck and the German Empire* (New York, 1968).
Howard, Michael, *The Franco–Prussian War* (New York, 1961).

Periodicals

Appleton's Journal
Atlanta Journal/Constitution
Harper's Weekly
The New York Herald
The New York Journal
The New York Times
New Yorker Staats-Zeitung

Index

Note: sub-entries under 'Salm-Salm, Prince Felix zu' and 'Salm-Salm, Princess Agnes zu' are chronological rather than alphabetical.

Alexander II, Tsar of Russia 147
Aquia Creek 28, 31
Atlanta (Georgia) 40, 49, 61, 62
Augusta, Queen of Prussia,
    German Empress 137, 138,
    140, 142, 144, 153, 177, 184

Bad Ems (Germany) 142, 143
Bancroft, George 136, 143
Basch, Dr Samuel 90, 91, 102,
    109, 112
Bazaine, General Achille 72, 73,
    77, 78, 79, 160, 163, 166
Benedetti, Count Vincente 151
Bennett, James Gordon 34
Birney, General David 30
Bismarck, Prince Otto von 121,
    136, 138, 150, 151
Blasio, José Luis 89, 90, 91, 92
Blenker, Colonel/General Louis
    5, 14, 16, 17, 18, 20, 21, 25
Blenker's Division 14, 17, 19, 20
Boer War 187
Bridgeport (Alabama) 38, 39
Brooks, Noah 9, 10, 29, 31
Bull Run, battles of 3, 4, 5, 6, 17,
    25
Burnside, General Ambrose E. 25,
    27
Busch, Dr Wilhelm 146, 147, 148,
    158, 159, 164, 168–73, 184

Carlota, Empress of Mexico 71,
    72, 73, 77, 84
Carol I, Prince of Rumania 135, 144
Cazadores (chasseurs) 83, 84, 85

Chattanooga, battle for 38, 50
Chattanooga (Tennessee) 37, 48
Coblenz (Germany) 141
Conscription Act (US) 36
Corvin, Colonel Otto von 26, 27,
    36, 52, 53, 55, 65, 133, 134,
    136, 153, 157, 164, 167, 184
Cox, Colonel 170, 172

Díaz, General Porfirio 73, 85, 90,
    94, 95, 96, 97, 122

8th New York Volunteers 17, 24,
    25, 27, 29, 32, 185, 186
Ems telegram 152
Escobedo, General Mariano 82,
    83, 89, 90, 91, 97, 107, 111,
    112, 113, 118

Faidherbe, General Louis 171,
    172, 173
Fenton, Governor Reuben 57
Forest, M. 107, 109
Franco–Prussian War
  deployment 156
  genesis 150
  German advance on
  outbreak 152
  battle of St Privat 161
  campaigns in northern France
    169ff
  capitulation at Sedan 165
  losses 173
  Metz 160
  Metz surrenders 166
  Paris capitulates 166, 173

Franz Joseph, Emperor of Austria 71, 72, 132, 133
Frémont, General John C. 19, 20, 21
Fritsch, Baron Friedrich Otto von 13, 35, 38, 41, 43, 53, 59, 63
Fry, Colonel/General James B. 37, 56, 57

Gerolt, Baron von 13, 16, 26, 31, 35, 64, 74, 121, 143, 181, 182
Goeben, General August von 170, 172, 174
Grant, General Ulysses S. 38, 58
Groeben, Captain von der 29, 48, 52, 56, 57, 74

Hall, Frederic 102, 105
Hans, Lieutenant Albert 84, 87
Harris, Senator Ira 23, 24, 37, 56
Heneage, Charles 183, 184
Hohenlohe-Ingelfingen, Prince Kraft von 136, 163, 166
Hohenzollern, Prince Karl Anton von 135, 144, 151, 184
Hohenzollern, Prince Karl von see Carol I of Rumania
Hohenzollern, Prince Leopold von 150, 151, 155
Hood, General John B. 40, 49, 51, 52, 61
Hooker, General Joseph 27, 29, 30, 31, 37, 38, 56
hospital and battlefield health care, US 46, 47
Hube family 93

Iglesias, José María 98, 99, 107
International Society 170
Isabella II, Queen of Spain 150

Jimmy, Agnes's terrier 34, 40, 41, 65, 95, 135, 143, 167, 170, 173, 178

Johnson, Delia (Agnes's sister) 3, 7, 55, 60, 63, 185
Johnson, Edmund 3, 55, 61
Johnson, Felix Salm-Salm (Agnes's nephew) 60, 63
Johnson, Frederick (Agnes's nephew) 184
Johnson, President Andrew 60, 64, 65, 114
Joy family 7, 9
Joy, Agnes Elizabeth Winona, see Salm-Salm, Princess Agnes zu
Juárez, President Benito 70, 71, 72, 73, 98, 99, 103, 107, 113, 114, 115

Krzyzanowksi, Colonel Wladimir 39, 50

Lago, Baron von 74, 107, 110, 118, 133
Lee, General Robert E. 25, 27, 36
Lincoln, Mrs Mary Todd 19, 31
Lincoln, President Abraham 3, 4, 14, 15, 20, 23, 31, 35, 36
López, Colonel Miguel 88, 90
Lyon, General Hylan B. 53, 54

Magnus, Baron Anton von 74, 75, 76, 77, 95, 96, 105, 106, 107, 109, 110, 116, 121, 122, 136
Malta, Knights of 154
Manteuffel, General Edwin von 169, 171, 173
Márquez, General Leonardo 77, 80, 81, 84, 85, 93, 94, 117
Martínez de la Torre, Rafael 102, 107, 114
Maximilian, Emperor of Mexico
  accepts throne 72
  arrives Mexico 72
  captured 89, 91
  character 85, 86

condemned 113
considers abdication 73, 77
escape plans 105, 109
executed 116
letter to Carlota 117
negotiations with Escobedo 101
prison conditions 102
to Querétaro 80
refuses to abandon his army 86, 87, 89
selection as emperor 71
trial 109
US attitude toward 108
McClellan, General George B. 3, 18, 19, 20, 25
Meagher, General Thomas F. 30, 52
Mejía, General Tomás 82, 86, 102, 109
Méndez, General Ramón 82, 86, 87, 91
Mexico
  Bazaine pulls out 73, 79
  Bazaine takes command 72
  Europeans land at Veracruz 71
  independence 69
  War of the Reform 70
Mexico City, life in 75, 76
Mexico–US War 1846–8, 4, 16, 69
Miramón, General Miguel 77, 81, 84, 86, 87, 88, 102, 109
Morgan, Governor Edwin D. 23, 24

Napoleon III, Emperor of the French 70, 71, 72, 73, 150, 151, 160, 165
Nashville, Battle of 51, 52
Nashville (Tennessee) 38, 40, 54
Nashville–Chattanooga Railroad 38, 39
New York draft riots 36

Oppenheim, Baron Edward 158, 168, 177, 178

Osuna, Duchess of (Eleanor zu Salm) 143, 147, 148, 182, 185
Otterburg, Marcus 121

Palacios, Colonel 102, 109, 110,111, 112
Pitner, Major/Colonel Ernst 83, 85, 87, 118
Pius IX, Pope 70, 179

Queen Augusta Regiment 137, 140, 151, 153, 166
Querétaro (Mexico)
  desperate situation in 89
  falls to Escobedo 89
  weakness of 80, 97

railways (US), importance of 38
Riva Palacio, Mariano 102, 107, 114
Rorschach (Switzerland) 134, 184
Runkel, Louise 155, 156, 157, 158, 163, 165, 167, 168, 169, 172, 173, 178, 181

St John, Knights of 154, 164
St-Privat, Battle of 161, 162
Salm family 11, 12, 130, 131
Salm-Salm, Prince Alfred (Felix's brother) 12, 121, 130, 132, 133, 154, 158, 163, 164, 168, 169, 173, 175, 181, 185
Salm-Salm, Prince Felix zu
  meets Agnes 5
  wedding 6, 21, 26
  birth and background 11
  in Prussian army 12
  arrives US 13
  interview with Lincoln 14
  on Blenker's staff 14, 19
  command of 8th New York Volunteers 24
  Corvin on 26

adjustment to US 26
at Aquia Creek 28
8th mustered out 32
in New York City 34
command of 68th New York
    Volunteers 34, 35
recruiting 35, 37
New York City draft riots 36
joins 68th in Bridgeport 37, 39
battle of Nashville 51, 52
commands reserve brigade 53
skirmishes 54, 55
praise from General Hooker 56
as brigadier general 58, 59
to Dalton, Georgia 59
commander Atlanta Military
    District 61
to Savannah 63
68th mustered out 63
sails for Mexico 64
arrives Veracruz 74
commissioned colonel 74
arrives Mexico City 75
to Querétaro 81
command of Cazadores 83
promotion 85
chief of Imperial Household 88
captured with emperor 89
negotiations with Escobedo 101
plans for escape 104, 106
commissioned general 104
plotting revealed 106
loyalty to emperor 116
sentenced 119, 120
departs Querétaro 120
imprisoned Mexico City 120
arrives Veracruz 122
sails for Europe 123
debt problems 132, 133
to Vienna and audience with
    Emperor Franz Joseph 132
Rorschach 134
received by King Wilhelm 136

Major, Queen Augusta Regiment
    137
joins regiment at Coblenz 139
continued extravagance 145
command of Fusiliers 147
regiment leaves for front 153
death 162
burial at Schloss Anholt 165
Salm-Salm, Prince Florentine
    (Felix's nephew) 153, 163, 165
Salm-Salm, Prince Leopold
    (Alfred's son) 155, 156, 164,
    173, 185
Salm-Salm, Princess Agnes zu
    meets Felix 5
    wedding 6
    birth and childhood 6
    circus 8
    Havana 8
    Felix and the 8th New York
        Volunteers 24
    in New York City 34
    recruitment for 68th New York
        Volunteers 37
    appointed captain 37
    to Bridgeport 41
    at home in Bridgeport 45
    hospital work 45, 47, 54, 63
    and Captain Fritsch 44, 53
    Lookout Mountain picnic 48
    campaign for Felix's promotion
        55–8
    to Dalton, Georgia 59
    President Johnson 60, 64, 65
    adopts nephew 60
    in Atlanta 61
    anger at Sherman 62
    to Savannah 63
    sails for Mexico 65
    arrives Veracruz 74
    on Mexican Indians 75
    arrives Mexico City 75
    on Bazaine 76

left by Felix in Mexico City 93
plans to rescue Maximilian and
    Felix 94, 95, 96
interview with Díaz 96
ordered out of Mexico 96
to Querétaro 97, 99
interviews with Juárez 98, 103
meets Maximilian 100
on Felix's escape plans 105
opinion of European ministers
    107
attempted plot with Colonel
    Palacios 111–12
expelled from Querétaro 112
pleads with Juárez 113, 115
to Veracruz and New York 123
sails for Europe 123
lands in France 129
arrives Schloss Anholt 130
Vienna 132
received by Archduchess Sophia
    133
awarded annuity 13
Rorschach 134
audience with Queen Augusta 137
to Coblenz 140
social whirl 143–4
growing discontent 144–6
begins hospital studies 149
childlessness 148–9
volunteers as nurse 152
licensed as nurse 155
off to the front 156
learns of Felix's death 163
finds his corpse 165
funeral 165
on Bazaine 166
back to hospital work 167
field work 168ff
returns to Schloss Anholt 175
Felix's debts again 175–6
decorated by emperor 177
appeals to Emperor Wilhelm 177

moves to Bonn 177
Switzerland 178
Italy 178
thoughts on entering convent
    179
interview with Pope Pius IX 179
saved by rich relative 181
Spain 182
book published 182
settles down in Bonn 182
marries Charles Heneage 183
returns regimental flags to New
    York 185–6
and Boer War 187
moves to Karlsruhe 188
death 188
Salm-Salm, Princess Eleanor see
    Osuna, Duchess of
Salm-Salm, Princess Wilhelmina
    ('Minna') 130, 153, 165, 175,
    185
Sanitary Commission (Germany)
    158, 164
Sanitary Commission (US) 46, 49
Savannah (Georgia) 57, 63
Schloss Anholt 130, 131
Schurz, Colonel Carl 16, 17, 40,
    186
Seward, William H. 14, 36, 73,
    114, 121
Seymour, Governor Horatio 34,
    35
Sherman, General William T. 38,
    40, 49, 61, 62
Sickles, General David E. 28, 31, 32
Sigel, Colonel/General Franz 16, 21
Simon, Frau 164, 165
68th New York Volunteers 34, 35,
    37, 38, 39, 63, 185–6
Sophia, Archduchess 78, 133
Spanish throne, candidacy for 150
Stahel, Colonel/General Julius 17,
    25, 27

Stanton, Edwin 20, 22, 36, 56, 57
Steedman, General James B. 40,
    48, 49, 50, 51, 52, 54, 56, 57,
    59, 63
Steinhausen, Colonel Albrecht
    von 35 37, 38, 43, 59
Steinmetz, General Karl Friedrich
    von 155, 156, 157, 168

Thomas, General George H. 40,
    49, 51, 57

Vidaurri, General Santiago 81, 82,
    85, 94, 117
Villaneuva, Colonel 100, 103, 109,
    110, 111, 112, 116

Wilhelm I, King of Prussia/
    German Emperor 136, 137,
    138, 143, 148, 151, 156, 158,
    160, 167, 184

Yates, Governor Richard 37, 57